D1810035

1 MONTH OF FREE READING

at

www.ForgottenBooks.com

By purchasing this book you are eligible for one month membership to ForgottenBooks.com, giving you unlimited access to our entire collection of over 1,000,000 titles via our web site and mobile apps.

To claim your free month visit:

www.forgottenbooks.com/free920210

ISBN 978-0-266-99186-1
PIBN 10920210

THE LEHIGH Alumni Bulletin

Beginning---

Life of Asa Packer

December, 1938

*Merry Christmas
Everybody...*

*...and to everybody
more smoking pleasure*

Chesterfield Cigarettes in their
attractive Christmas cartons
appeal to everyone. Their
refreshing *mildness* and *better
taste* give smokers everywhere
more pleasure.

Chesterfield *They Satisfy*

Engineer

Alumnus of the month is a man whose work is seen in the Grand Coulee dam, the Fort Peck diversion tunnels and the new Lincoln tunnels under the Hudson river. Here is a sketch of his activities as an engineer with his own description of the newest tube project.

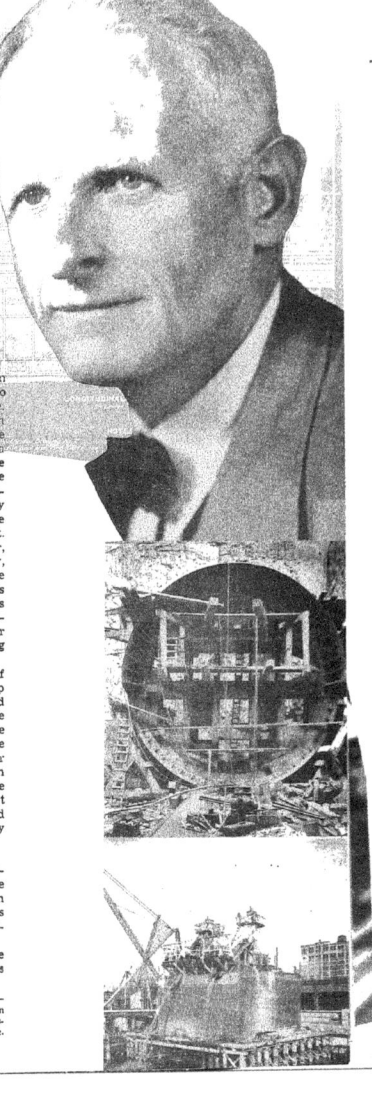

THINGS have been going down for one Francis Donaldson ever since he graduated from Lehigh University in 1901 with the degree of mechanical engineer. And yet the very success of the going down process has made this same Mr. Donaldson outstanding in his field for as a construction engineer there are few that can equal him and most of the projects that have felt his guiding hand have involved going down—into the earth from one point to another regardless of what might stand in the way.

Had Varied Schooling

Probably his taking up of the transit and blue-print was as much a surprise to his Scotch-Irish parents as to anyone else, for his father and grandfather before him had been physicians and when he was born in Howard County, Md., August 11, 1881, if any future were planned for him it must have centered on the career of medicine. But it was in New York at Halsey School that he began his education, and soon the scene changed from 38th Street to Surbiton, England, and then a return to Concord, N. H. where the St. Paul's School offered him a preparatory education.

It was from Baltimore, Maryland that he entered Lehigh University at the age of 16 where he found little trouble in negotiating his studies and at the same time taking a part in extra curricular activities. In his Junior year he was a member of the varsity track team, gymnasium team, and took part in the Junior oratorical contest. By his senior year he was vice-president of Tau Beta Pi, a member of the Phi Club and Kappa Kappa and took part in the minstrel show. He joined the Delta Phi social fraternity.

Meanwhile, a decade earlier, two other Lehigh men, Frank and Ralph Dravo, had begun the fabricating firm in Pittsburgh which was to grow to huge proportions and bear their name. It was to this company that Donaldson looked after his graduation at the age of 20 years, and there he began as a construction engineer, a title which he was to carry until the present time. He served as chief engineer for the company from 1907 to 1912 and already had a taste of underground work in the construction of the Catskill Aqueduct. In the latter year, as chief engineer, he joined the T. A. Gillespie Company, a firm which was involved in the same project. Two years later, he had his first experience in the subway field as engineer for three large subway projects in the City of New York under the aegis of the Degnan Contracting Company.

The War found him active in behalf of his country's hectic drive to set up cantonments and shipyards in record time, and at the close of hostilities he went into business for himself in the consulting line until 1927 when he joined the firm of Mason and Hanger as chief engineer. Under his direction the New Jersey Foundation for the George Washington Bridge was brought into being and four tubes were pushed into the East River for another subway project in New York.

Aided With Coulee Dam

Then with the Mason-Walsh-Atkinson-Kier Company, he aided in the construction of the Grand Coulee Dam and later with Mason and Walsh was chief engineer on the Fort Peck diversion tunnels.

But Francis Donaldson was not one to allow the demanding duties of his

(Continued on page twenty-one)

Above, Francis Donaldson. Center, test section of Lincoln tunnel as erected by engineers. Below, terminal section being sunk to meet the tube.

IN 1912, a high tower with chutes was used for the placement and transportation of concrete at Dam No. 15, Ohio River

Typical of Dravo Progress During the Last Twenty-five Years

IN 1937, a modern marine mixing plant and traveling whirlers were used for concreting at Gallipolis Dam, Ohio River.

Our Alumni

———o———

S. P. Felix, '03

J. D. Berg, '05

E. T. Gott, '06

A. S. Osbourne, '09

L. C. Zollinger, '09

V. B. Edwards, '12

Geo. F. Wolfe, '14

W. P. Berg, '17

E. H. Zollinger, '18

F. J. Lloyd, Jr., '23

B. E. Rhoads, '23

J. A. Bissinger, Jr., '26

W. W. Armstrong, '27

R. W. Marvin, '27

Paul G. Strohl, '27

G. W. Fearnside, Jr., '28

Stanley B. Adams, '29

C. W. Granacher, '29

E. V. Twiggar, '31

J. K. Beidler, '34

W. A. Robinson, '34

H. E. Lore, '35

L. P. Struble, Jr., '35

R. Parsons, '38

Letters to the Editor

"One Constructive Step"

Dear Mr. Parsons:

As a student, alumnus and faculty member, and as former sports publicity director (Feb. 1936-June 1938), I have watched Lehigh students and athletes since September 1927. The present agitation which the record of the 1938 football team aroused seems to be as futile as all other waves of agitation have been at Lehigh, because, in my opinion, it does not get to the seat of the trouble.

One constructive step might be a more determined effort to keep the athletes that we now have in school. Year after year promising players go on probation for lack of tutoring or close scholastic supervision.

If Lehigh is to have successful athletic teams without sacrificing Lehigh standards of scholarship, Lehigh or Lehigh alumni must secure a scholastic coach for her athletes. By this, I don't mean someone who merely checks on their grades as Westerman and Calvert do now or someone who runs a brief course as the Education department is doing, but someone who will keep on the trail of these boys and be father, brother, coach and teacher all at the same time. Such a man could raise sufficiently the grades of most Lehigh athletes to keep them off probation.

The result would not end here. Today, many athletes hesitate to come to Lehigh because they are afraid of flunking out. Each time an athlete flunks out his failure discourages other athletes from coming. Then too most athletes realize that it takes more than one man to make a team; so they go where other athletes go. In other words, the more athletes a college has; the more it gets.

I would be glad to discuss other angles of this plan with you either by mail or at any time you may be in Bethlehem.

Very truly yours,
KENNETH K. KOST, '31.

"I Can't Take It"

Dear Bob:

It has been about two years, Bob, since I dashed off a long and passionate discourse on one (1) the advantages of being a Lehigh graduate and two (2) why we should rehire Glen Harmeson as football coach. As for the first, if

The Lehigh Alumni Bulletin

Official publication of
The Lehigh Alumni Association

President, Floyd W. Parsons, '02; Vice-Presidents, R. G. Johnson, '04 and J. J. Shiphard, '21; Treasurer, R. S. Taylor, '95; Executive Secretary, Wm. A. Cornelius, '89.

ALUMNUS TRUSTEES
Alexander Potter, '90; Robert Farnham, '99; Morton Sultzer, '12; Frank B. Bell, '97; Daniel Berg, '05; and Andrew E. Buchanan, Jr., '18.

BULLETIN Committee: A. W. Hicks, Jr., '23, Chairman, Cosmopolitan; G. F. Nordenholt, '14, Product Engineering; M. A. DeWolfe Howe, '86. Atlantic Monthly, retired; E. G. Hoar, '35, Conde Nast Publications; J. I. Kirkpatrick, '29.

Published monthly, October to June, inclusive, by the Alumni Association of Lehigh University, Inc., Alumni Memorial Building, Bethlehem, Pa. Printed by the Lehigh Printing Corporation Bethlehem, Pa. Entered as second-class matter at Bethlehem, Pa. Post Office. Subscription price, $3.00 per year. National advertising representatives The Graduate Group, Inc., New York, New York, Chicago, Detroit, San Francisco, Los Angeles and Boston.

VOL. XXVI—NUMBER 3   DECEMBER, 1938

you analyze contents of said letter, I'm still of the opinion of the first part heartily and in deep agreement on everything I said and what the school stands for and does.

I regret, though, that I ever suggested anything about rehiring Harmy as coach. In the first place, Harmy will ruin himself if he stays any longer and I wouldn't blame him for resigning this year.

I've got to admit it but I just can't take a whipping any longer. I feel sincerely either we ought to fish or cut bait, either we are going to have a good little team or not have any team at all—quit the game cold and frankly admit it. I believe in being Simon Pure up to a certain point and then after that, no! When the time comes that all we can win is from Johns Hopkins, P. M. C., and Delaware—well, that's the payoff.

Here's what I propose:

1. Penn State, Lafayette. Rutgers, Muhlenberg are natural rivals.

2. Case, Boston U. could be made into rivals of the best type as witness the three Case games and the two Boston U. games.

3. This makes up a six-game list right there with two opens for others. This would be an attractive schedule for all — students and alumni.

4. In this league we would be in our own backyard and playing in our own class.

5. With teams such as Harmy put out in his first three years we could win as an average 50 per cent of the home and home games. Some years would be better than others.

6. No man on those teams of '34 to '36 ever disgraced the school—none were tramp athletes.

7. Let us offer scholarships either board, room or tuition to fellows of that type who can play football, are willing to study—perhaps not engineering but business or arts—those that desire can take engineering and let's have a team.

Now this may be futile but I think it's worth trying. Last year can be discounted. Harmy had a swell line but no backs—this year he has nothing. I'm in favor of asking him and Westerman to go out and get this needed material. He knows how far the school will go and no further. Certainly Lehigh men are good men and in general above the field however in my very brief business career I've met some pretty damn good engineers from Cornell, Purdue, Wisconsin. Michigan and others. We have no corner on that. Now those schools go a hell of a lot further in getting athletes than what I've just proposed.

I'm not asking that all six of those schools on our rival list be beaten every year. I'm asking that Lafayette, Penn State, Rutgers, etc., be beaten every other year. If you will check over attendance records of the Lafayette games of '34, '35, '36, I think you'll see that more alumni came back than last year—many solely to see Lafayette beaten. I'm not thinking of the dollar sign, either, but if you're asking for alumni to come back and see the school and give toward new buildings, how about giving them some satisfaction of seeing Lafayette beaten and being able to see in the Sunday paper where we did win or gave some one in our class a hell of a tough fight. I think there are many who agree with me—maybe not. But I can't take it anymore. If we are going to be another M. I. T. then let's quit sports altogether.

Sincerely,
E. S. GALLAGHER, '34.

"Situation Is Serious"

Dear Sir:

I wish to express my appreciation for your recent article in the LEHIGH ALUMNI BULLETIN upon the athletic situation and to add our opinion that the situation is serious requiring alumni action. As an officer of the Central Pennsylvania

Lehigh Club for several years I have listened to many complaints from our alumni who are made to feel their alma mater is a prep school because of its low grade athletics. Many of our prominent alumni feel this keenly and are strong in the opinion Lehigh should abolish football if they can not compete with colleges of their class.

We have have several investigating committees who only report the majority of athletes come from families who can not afford to send their sons to college and therefore we can not interest them in Lehigh unless we can offer them the same kind of help that our competing colleges offer. As a solution of this problem I wish to present the following suggestion for consideration.

The Lehigh Fund can be divided among several objectives such as new equipment, endowment, and student aid, each alumnus being privileged to contribute to the objective he desires to support. Those of us who desire to support student aid with the thought we are helping worthy boys to secure an education would contribute towards alumni scholarships, the number to be limited and depend upon the amount of money contributed for this purpose.

The scholarships should be sufficient to cover tuition and room rent in the dormitories. The University should be asked to assist by giving a reduced rate which assistance could come from a reduction in the number of regional scholarships. The scholarships should meet University regulations but the awards should be made by an alumni committee and in the local alumni district which contribute the money for the scholarship. The local alumni committee could also follow the boy with whatever additional help is needed such as employment during summer vacations.

I believe it is the duty of our alumni to do something to restore Lehigh's reputation in the athletic world and that some action should be formulated in time to assist boys entering next year's class. If nothing can be done then I would join the large group of alumni who believe we should confine our football to the campus.

Very truly yours,
CLASS OF '22.

"Delighted Beyond Measure"

Dear Floyd:

My LEHIGH ALUMNI BULLETIN came this morning, and I did not delay reading your article "Football Policy." It delighted me beyond measure, as I am one of those who have been getting all you mention in your article, but never knew to whom I could voice my complaints regarding Lehigh Athletics, and especially football. It has always seemed to me that the Alumni have been strangely indifferent to all this, but perhaps its members have had the same difficulty that I mention in that they did not know what to do about it. I have from time to time mentioned the lamentable showing of our teams to Lehigh men with whom I have been in correspondence, but this is as far as I could get.

Every fall I have more or less frothed at the mouth over this situation, and it has become an annual condition with me. I have become rather tired of being urged to attend the Lafayette game, to see, year after year, the glorious Lehigh team go down to valiant defeat. It is pitiful, as these boys work just as hard as they do anywhere else and with apparently the same loyalty, and all they get of it is to be banged around by every college or school that happens to be on the schedule. I am also tired of constantly hearing that nothing must be done that will in any way detract from Lehigh's notably high standard. I am not one to say that it should, and I do not believe the Alumni in general ever have had this thought in mind. It is beginning to sound like a sort of alibi. I see no reason why having a reasonably good football team must necessarily reduce the standard of any institution. Why should this be peculiar to Lehigh alone; there are many colleges in the country that enjoy very

(Continued on page fifteen)

"Isn't this where we came in?

Behind the *J*

One of the oldest stories in the world is college athletics—clean or unclean, white or black as coal. Probably the Greeks in their universities centuries ago wrestled with this problem. So there is nothing particularly new about what we are here discussing.

Before the turn of the century I was yelling at Lafayette for having borrowed the year before the left tackle of the West Virginia football team to use him in their game against Pennsylvania the following Saturday. I was then at West Virginia and our tackle returned to us, sound and safe, with a little gift remembrance. Shortly afterwards, he became one of the most famous coaches in the country and is still an outstanding figure.

But we were not so pure ourselves at Lehigh in those days, and many of us helped to bring in good players, some of whom managed to stick it out and graduate. When captain of the Lehigh baseball team, I remember very well playing our own coach in a game against North Carolina merely because when we got down there we discovered they intended to play their coach, so it was tit for tat.

In recent weeks, I have read so many letters from Lehigh graduates and discussed this athletic question with such a great number of them that I have now reached that state of saturation which makes it difficult to know from what angle or end to begin. Perhaps the first and primary statement should be that we are all mighty fond of our University and desire to avoid any and all actions that will prove destructive or divide us into schools of bitter thought.

Professors Are Helpful

Certainly we will get nowhere by being partisan, narrow-minded, or unfair. Some of the faculty cry harder and louder when we lose a game than any of the rest of us. Some of the staunchest supporters of a policy of having winning teams are teaching at Lehigh, and these men I know do give of their time and effort to help athletes who are having a struggle. It is unnecessary to point out the fallacy in the idea, if there is such an idea, that the faculty as a whole is responsible for our football heartaches.

On the other hand, it is doubtless true that there are spots in the University's teaching staff where some educational work concerning athletics might be carried on with profit. Boys who are spending much time in training can be helped a lot by those departments that are ready and willing to go to reasonable limits in re-arranging schedules, etc. I know personally several professors who have gone to all reasonable limits trying to help members of the teams.

It really is not my job to editorialize about remedies. My conception of the duty of the president of the Alumni Association is that he should seek above all else to confine his efforts to acting merely as a spokesman for the best opinion of a large majority of the graduates. Of course, he must present the problem in a true light, and here it is in the fewest possible words.

We have gone through several periods of good teams and bad teams. In years past, money has been appropriated by Alumni to get athletes into Lehigh and keep them there. We had a Student Aid Fund, and theoretically this was ideal. Every name of those being helped was published, and Lafayette or any other college could have these names. But for various reasons that need not now be discussed, this Fund was killed off, and "Slim" Wilson, who was back East from California the other day, had lunch with me and recited the details of what happened, and why.

A lot of Lehigh men who would give their right arms to see our football boys trim all rivals have had some mighty unhappy experiences. I have heard many of the old stories about help that was promised and failed to materialize; about tough guys who were sent to Bethlehem to help us win games and turned out to be "sick headaches"; and about dozens of other mistakes that finally caused a lot of Alumni, especially in Bethlehem, to develop what now comes close to being a defeatist attitude. Men like Walter Okeson, Bob Taylor, Dick Dodson, Gene Grace and others who rank second to none in their approval of victorious teams have doubtless had plenty of hours of misery in their dealings with the problem here being discussed.

Like a lot of other Lehigh graduates who have been on the outside looking in, I was unfamiliar with the details of what has already been done at Lehigh as well as the details of what is being done today at other high-class colleges. For that reason I started with an open mind and have been seeking to get my education at the very foundation of learning. I have here before me the statements that have been made respecting athletics by Lehigh presidents, faculty members, and prominent alumni for the past 40 or 50 years, and these opinions are extremely interesting and enlightening. They bear out the first statement I made in this article, which was that the story is an old one.

Graduates Favor Help

It is already plain that some of the athletes who were brought to Lehigh and given help turned out to be fine students. I could mention 10 or 12 names to make the point undeniable. It is also evident that Lehigh graduates practically as a whole are in favor of extending help to promising athletes by various methods that are entirely legitimate. A lot of the hullabaloo about subsidation is rather confusing for the simple reason that different people have different ideas concerning the true meaning of the word.

I think I have said enough in the foregoing to carry this discussion another step forward. From here on it is going to be necessary to have the BULLETIN present a fairly wide cross-section of all classes of opinion. I do not have permission to publish the contents of all of the letters that have come to me. In fact, there would be very little space left in the BULLETIN for anything else if the comments so far submitted were published in full. However, I believe it will be helpful right now to set forth brief extracts from some of the letters received in order that the reader may gather some idea respecting the spirit that prevails.

First of all, I feel confident that every Lehigh man will be interested in the thoughts contained in a letter I received from President Williams. As those who know Dr. Williams would naturally expect, he is sympathetic with intercollegiate sports. After pointing out that many of the intimations about faculty members being unduly hard on athletes, on investigation, are frequently discovered to be unfounded, he went on to say:

"I have been rather intimately in-

Going deeper into Lehigh's football history, the author finds reasons why some alumni hail the past years and others regret them

tball Picture

BY
FLOYD W.
PARSONS
President, Lehigh Alumni Association

volved in the administration of athletics at three large state universities, as chairman of eligibility for a number of years at two. I know that the most erudite professor with the least apparent interest in athletics shares the joy when his college team wins, and any professor that I have ever known would always give an athlete the benefit of the doubt in grading a paper. I myself have always been thoroughly sympathetic with athletics, yet there have been times when as chairman of the Eligibility Committee, honesty compelled me to declare a prominent athlete ineligible.

"I am confident that there is not a teacher at Lehigh who would not be eminently fair towards an athlete, yet grading of scholastic work must be made as objective in standards as practicable. I should think it would be well if some qualified alumnus would review a case some time where lack of sympathy with an athlete is alleged to exist and report his findings. I have never known of an effort being made to ascertain the facts in such a case, because the rumor seems the more pleasing to believe."

List Alumni Comments

Here follow other comments from alumni. A past president of the Lehigh Club of Western New York says: "A good football team is a decided asset to any university. For years I have suggested athletic scholarships for good football players who are equally good students. I believe you would find many donations made to an athletic fund in the same manner as the response of the alumni to the Alumni Endowment Fund. The secretary of the Lehigh Club of Western New York was instructed to write you that our group is 100 percent behind the airing of the athletic situation."

From a member of the Class of '21 comes this: "Record my resounding vote of approval for plan to determine an appropriate football policy. Many of us have been interested in the other sports such as baseball, basketball, wrestling, soccer, lacrosse, tennis, and track, that are presumably financed by the gate receipts of football. As these sports at Lehigh have consequently suffered from the neglect of football. I would be in favor of any plan by which the whole athletic program could be rehabilitated. Some members of the faculty may better be described as unpatronizing rather than unsympathetic. In certain spots there appears to be positively no understanding of the social value of public athletic attractions upon the academic lives of young people.

"Right now we have an exceptionally able group of coaches in such men as Harmeson, Sheridan, Calvert, Carpenter, Morrissey, Mercur, and Kanaly. By inducing men with a modicum of athletic experience to come to Lehigh and by giving them considerable treatment thereafter, a satisfactory program can be maintained without lowering scholastic standards or signing tramp athletes. If you will read President Williams' comments in the article called "The Prexy's Pen" on Page 18 of the November 1937 issue of The Alumni BULLETIN, it might be concluded that lack of funds for such purposes was the main reason for our failure to support teams in better fashion."

I thought I could include excerpts

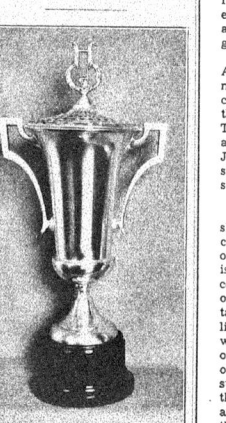

Award

PRESENTED by the New York Lehigh Club, the cup above is to be awarded for the intramural group singing in a contest to be held on the Lehigh campus during the coming spring.

In an effort to foster singing by fraternity and dormitory groups, officers of the New York Club have donated the award and a committee, headed by Morton Sultzer, '12, has contacted the student body to arrange details.

from ten or fifteen letters, but in trying to do this I find that I am leaving out so many things of interest and importance that the letters are really spoiled. Furthermore, the space available for this article has been largely exhausted, so let me merely present a few high spots from current comments before closing:

"A lot of us who are crabbers have never looked about and tried to get a good athlete into Lehigh."

"Frequently our teams are licked before the game starts. One reason is the attitude of the town and the college."

Lehigh is a great University. It has been able to forge ahead even with poor teams. Lafayette's fine teams did not help them very much. Nevertheless, in spite of the fact that Lehigh, even during the depression has never been in the red, the college would be better off, our student body would be improved, and the alumni would be much happier if we could make a better showing in athletics. A lot of fine boys who are not athletes are drawn to colleges where they have good teams.

"We have very few scholarships. Might we not have more? I believe it is true that you cannot make good football players. Those who have had experience assert that they are born, and that means you must go out and get them."

"Suggest the appointment of an Alumni committee to interview alumni of other colleges who are in Lehigh's class, and in this way, determine how they handle their athletic problems. This committee might make a report and recommendations for action at the June Alumni Meeting. Make haste slowly and sanely. I know the Lehigh situation can be improved."

Number Would Contribute

"Certainly we should make a better showing with institutions of our own class, and it appears to me that the only solution in the getting of material is help from the Alumni. The Alumni contribute generously to the support of the institution in helping to maintain its academic standards, and I believe there are a large number who would gladly contribute to the support of the athletic teams. I happen to know of a plan that has worked at other institutions where a certain number of the Alumni pledge comparatively small amounts each year for the support of their teams, and while I realize that this cannot be a formal policy of the "Alumni Association" or the University, it has its merits, and I know from experience that it has produced results. Such a fund could be used to great advantage in providing good athletes with a good education at a college where the educational facilities are the best."

All of the foregoing represents a rough cross-section of the current opinions of Lehigh graduates. Some of the letters I have received are three and four pages long and they not only go into minute details respecting plans, but they also deal with many questions that cannot be handled in haste.

Lehigh Clubs throughout the country are now taking up this matter and many of them are passing resolutions. Whatever any of us may feel concerning this highly important and controversial question, it is true beyond any shadow of doubt that the moment had arrived to let off a bit of steam, and I am sure the Lehigh engine will function more safely and efficiently because of the attention being given this problem. I'll appreciate your comments and suggestions sent adong to me at 32 West 40th Street N. Y. City, or send them to Robert Herrick, editor of the BULLETIN.

The Directors Look Ahead

At their annual fall meeting, chairmen of the alumni committees report on all phases of graduate activity, seek completion of fund drive.

By

Wm. A. Cornelius

Executive Secretary, the Lehigh Alumni Association

THE report of an Association that continued to hold its own in the face of existing economic circumstances was read before the Board of Directors of the Alumni Association when they gathered for their annual fall meeting on Saturday November 19 prior to the Lehigh-Lafayette Game.

In all phases of the Alumni Association work, headed by committeemen who had gathered to give reports of the activities of their groups, progress was shown toward the goal of aiding the University through the work of its graduates. The Directors look forward to a successful conclusion of their drive to finance the Harry M. Ullmann Wing of the chemistry laboratory which is being completed this year and if funds yet to be collected are gathered prior to the general meeting of the Alumni Association in June, the consensus of opinion seemed to point to a new project for activity on the part of Lehigh graduates.

Minutes of Meeting

In detail minutes of the meeting are as follows:

The meeting was called to order at 11:00 a. m. by F. W. Parsons,'02, President. Those present were F. W. Parsons, R. G. Johnson, '04, R. S. Taylor, '95, A. A. Diefenderfer, '02, A. E. Buchanan, Jr., '18, W. R. Okeson, '95, W. H. Lesser, '05, A. W. Hicks, Jr., '23, C. S. Kenney, '10, R. F. Herrick, '34 and William A. Cornelius, '89. Alexander Potter '90 sent a telegram advising he could not be present; Robert Farnham, '99 could not be on hand due to the fact that he had a large party of guests to take care of; Morton Sultzer, '12 and J. J. Shipherd, '21 notified the Executive Secretary by telephone of their inability to be present. During the course of the meeting John I. Kirkpatrick, '29, whose duty it will be to look after endowment for the University, dropped in on invitation from the Executive Secretary. He was introduced by the chairman and briefly stated his pleasure at being able to help in this work. He said he had already gotten a lot of data from E. F. Johnson but still had a lot to learn and would be coming to Bethlehem on December 1 to take over his duties.

On motion, the minutes of the last meeting, June 10, 1938, as printed in Alumni Bulletin, were formally approved.

The President called on the Executive Secretary for his report. He announced that things were moving along nicely in the office and in the Alumni Association. Compared with this same time last year, there are 17 more paying alumni dues, 91 more subscribing to the Bulletin, and counting the promises to be paid during this academic year, there are only 12 less contributors to the Alumni Fund for this period. This has all been without any personal, face to face solicitation and in spite of rather poor financial conditions throughout the country. The Executive Secretary went on to say that he might have other things to discuss regarding what would likely come up in remarks of Standing Committee Chairmen. He suggested the meeting go right ahead with old business and reports of these committees.

The President called on A. C. Dodson, '00, to report on the Alumni Fund and Mr. Dodson presented a written report which he read in full. The Fund Chairman said in part that up to November 17 a sizable sum had been paid over to the University from the Fund for the addition to the chemistry laboratory. None the less, he pointed out an appreciable balance remained to be paid in order that the Alumni Association's promise of $150,000 on this project be completed by June. He bespoke the help not only of the Directors but of the entire alumni body in this connection.

A. W. Hicks, Jr., '23, reported very briefly on the Alumni Bulletin, stating that R. F. Herrick, '34, Editor, was present with a full report on the subject. Herrick then presented a written report the substance of which was as follows:

Shows Advertising Loss

"Due to heavy losses in advertising in the national field, a matter which is controlled solely by our national advertising representatives, Bulletin revenue in the advertising field has not shown the gains that might be expected. In the month of October, a gain of $93.00 was shown over the previous year, and in November $22.33. These gains allowed for compensation of loss in national advertising which has been overcome by advertising solicitations through the Bulletin office.

"Circulation showed a loss of 74 subscribers over last year with the October edition, whereas the November issue showed a gain of 16 subscribers over the same month last year.

"The policy of reinvesting Bulletin profits has been continued with the net profit to date being held at the low figure of $116.25 for the first two issues. Over 1,000 pieces of first class mail have been sent out in October and to date 600 have been mailed in November.

"As the Bulletin committee is made up of men whose activities are unusually limited by demanding positions in New York, it has been possible to hold but one meeting of the Bulletin committee but this was a most successful one and resulted in valuable counsel to Bulletin editors. Another meeting is planned for December."

Alexander Potter, '90 sent in a written report on Alumni Homecoming Day and called attention to the program which included the inspection of the Charles Russ Richards House, the conferences held by the Deans of the three colleges, and the reception to the class of '92 as honored guests of the University, celebrating fifty years since they

(Continued on page nineteen)

A Wing Opens

Into the Harry M. Ullmann annex to the chemistry laboratory come new equipment and renewed activity as
all classes find the most advanced facilities for the
theory and practice of a popular engineering course.

4

5

6

7

As classes opened in the new Harry M. Ullmann chemistry wing, financed by contributions from Lehigh alumni, the activities shown on this page were seen. (1) A professor instructs a class in the new lecture room. (2) Apparatus from semi-commercial countercurrent absorption study. (3) Seniors work in the new chemical engineering laboratory. (4) Dr. Anderson instructs in the use of X-ray equipment. (5) Reverse view of chemical engineering laboratory. (6) Memorial plaque to Homer D. Williams room dedicated by Mrs. Clara S. Williams. (7) Typical private laboratory and office. (8) Freshmen conduct their experiments in this elementary chemistry laboratory.

8

We begin the story of Asa Packer not on a December day of 1805, at the home of his fathers in New England, but on a sunny Indian Summer afternoon of October 1938, in a country cemetery on a Pennsylvania hillslope overlooking his beloved Mauch Chunk.

Here, in imagination, we join a small group, headed by the distinguished President of a great University, paying homage to a great man by the simple ceremony of placing a wreath of laurel at his final resting place.

In the gorge below lie the winding river, the abandoned canal, the busy railroad; all of the name of Lehigh, which were Asa Packer's domain for half a century. Far down the valley, on another hillside overlooking the river, stands Asa Packer's College, also bearing the name Lehigh. Here, on the morning of the same day, in Asa Packer's Church, the faculty, students, and friends of the college assembled, as they have each recurring October for sixty years, to honor the Founder.

Our scene now shifts backward to 1879, where, from across the years, the Railroad built by Asa Packer joins its tribute to that of the college he founded. May I read these paragraphs from the minutes of the meeting of the Board of Directors of the Lehigh Valley Railroad Company, held June 10, 1879.

Directors Mark Sorrow

"The Directors of the Lehigh Valley Railroad Company, have heard with profound sorrow the death of their President, the Honorable Asa Packer; by which each one of the Directors has lost a true and valued friend, the Company has lost its founder and its sagacious leader, the laboring man has lost a sympathizing benefactor, and our country has lost a useful and patriotic citizen.

"Our present point of view being from this council board, it would not be suitable to dwell on his personal qualities, his purity of life, the uprightfulness of his dealings, the simplicity, dignity and integrity of his character, his freedom from all assumption and ostentation, his large and enlightened liberality, his firmness, his self-acquired and skillfully applied knowledge, and the perserverance and sagacity by which he honorably acquired distinction and wealth, not by

Here in country cemetery begins the first chapter of a serial devoted to the life of Lehigh's founder---The human story of a man who stood out in industry, politics and character.

By

Milton C. Stuart

Professor of Mechanical Engineering

ADAPTED FROM A SPEECH BEFORE THE NEWCOMEN SOCIETY BY PERMISSION.

taking that wealth away from somebody else, but by creating it. It is not for us to intrude into the sanctity of his tender domestic relations, or his reverent worship of his God."

Born at Mystic, New London County, Connecticut, December 29, 1805, the boy attended the winter district school, and worked in a tannery and on a farm. Seeing no future here, he determined to seek his fortune in other parts. Thus we catch our first significant glimpse of Asa Packer in 1882 as a youth of 17, setting out on foot from his ancestral home in Connecticut for the frontier forests in the upper reaches of the Susquehanna. The record is not clear, but with a biographer's imagination, I picture the tall young Asa, knapsack on back, swinging across New Jersey, perhaps along the future route of the Morris Canal, into the Lehigh Valley, past Bethlehem and past Mauch Chunk, over the mountains to Berwick and up the Susquehanna to Brooklyn, Susquehanna County.

The goal was the home of an uncle, Edward Packer, a carpenter by trade to whom Asa apprenticed himself. This movement of the Packer family from Connecticut to Pennsylvania was but a continuation of an earlier migration from the Nutmeg State to the Wyoming region of Northeastern Pennsylvania. Here he spent ten years in a manner not dissimilar to that which history records of another great American of the time; felling trees, clearing land, building cabins of log, following his trade of carpentry in the winter, and of farming in the summer.

Here, on January 23, 1828, Asa married Sarah Blakeslee, who throughout a long life shared his hardships and successes, his poverty and wealth, living to celebrate with Asa the Golden Wedding.

The feeling of Mr. Packer towards his wife at the close of his career, as well as insight into his character, is given by one item in his last Will and Testament, a document which covered 21 printed pages and in minute detail disposed of an estate variously estimated to have a potential value of from 6 to 20 million dollars.

The first paragraph of the Will reads:

"I hereby give, devise and bequeath to my wife, Sarah M. Packer, such part of my estate, real and personal, principal and income, as she may at any time during her life-time desire, wish or select. This is to be hers absolutely, and the trustees are hereby authorized, empowered and directed, at any time or times, when she shall request them so to do, to pay, hand over and transfer to her any property or money, whether principal or income, according to her wishes and directions. Should she choose to indicate at any time what she wishes set apart for herself out of the principal, or as an annual income, the trustees may do so in accordance with her wishes, and may then administer the remainder of the trust as herein directed. My purpose is that she shall have whatever she wishes out of my estate, and all other provisions hereof are subordinate to this one." It should be stated here that the Widow never had occasion to avail herself of this provision.

Stirred by Industry

But now while the stout arms and axe of her carpenter husband are clearing the woodland her nimble fingers and spinning wheel are preparing every garment for the household need.

But Asa Packer was not to remain a humble worker in forest and field. In 1833, at the age of 28, impelled by the stirrings of new industry, he moves to the valley of the Lehigh, and his career begins. In order to understand this career, which was associated at first with coal and canals, and later with a railroad, it is essential that we recall the industrial and transportation situation in 1833 in the Lehigh Valley and environs.

The romantic story of the discovery of Anthracite coal in Pennsylvania, and the early attempts to get it to burn and to market it need not be retold here. But it is necessary to recount how in 1812, Colonel George Shoemaker of Pottsville, took nine wagon loads of coal to Philadelphia, sold two loads and was obliged to give away the other seven for want of buyers. One of the two loads was purchased by Josiah White who operated a wire mill at Schuylkill Falls. If we were not presenting the life of a Connecticut Yankee, we should like to digress to tell the thrilling story of the Philadelphia Quaker, Josiah White, who went into the wilds of the Upper Lehigh, established the Lehigh Coal and Navigation Company in 1817-1820, made the Lehigh navigable, and built the Lehigh Canal from Mauch Chunk to the Delaware.

The decade of the 1820's saw not only the completion of the Erie Canal, but the great network of waterways built to carry the black diamonds to the Metropolitan markets. These were the Delaware and Hudson Canal built by Maurice Wurtz, the Schuylkill Canal, the North Branch Canal on the Susquehanna, the Delaware Canal south of Easton, the Morris Canal across New Jersey and our Lehigh Canal which was opened for tolls in 1829.

The Mauch Chunk Railroad was built by the Lehigh Canal and Navigation Company, under the direction of Josiah White, in 1827, for the purpose of bringing coal down to the canal. The rails were of wood, covered with strips of iron ore and one half inches thick. The coal cars came down by gravity and mules were used to haul the empty cars back up to the mines. The story is told that when the mules became accustomed to riding down in style in empty cars, with refreshments provided, only with difficulty could they be persuaded to go down any other way. This railroad

(Continued on page seventeen)

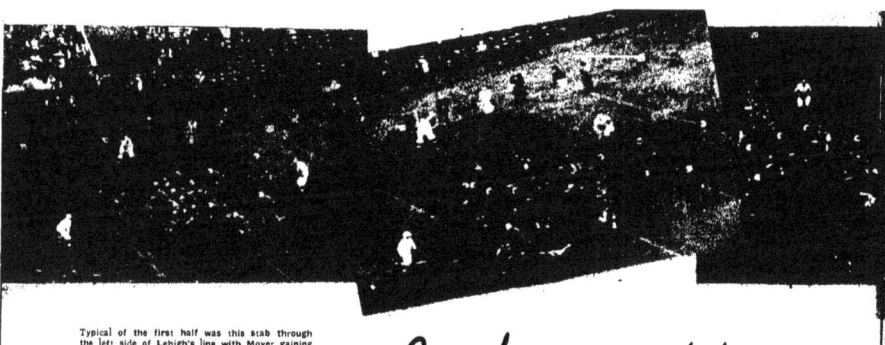

Lafayette, 6

A fighting Lehigh team battled with
determination against New York University and Muhlenberg elevens, but
reached its peak in the final game of
the season against a highly favored
Lafayette powerhouse. Although these
three opponents were far superior in
quality and quantity of experienced
players, the Brown and White combination, facing student and alumni
criticism, improved with each game
and upset the dopesters who predicted
a one-sided Lafayette victory.

Lafayette, 6; Lehigh, 0

Only high praise has been sung in
honor of the Engineers as they
emerged from a close 6-0 defeat handed
them by the Lafayette Leopards in the
72nd game of the longest and one of
the oldest rivalries in American gridiron history on Nov. 19.

Caught asleep in the initial quarter,
the Brown and White team was sucked
in by a reverse play which enabled
George Moyer, sophomore substitute
back from Phillipsburg, N. J. to skirt
down the field for 32 yards and the
only touchdown of the afternoon as
close to 8,000 loyal rooters sat through
a driving rainstorm.

Aside from this dash down the field,
the Leopards were completely outclassed by Harmeson's inspired eleven.
The Engineers' line proved impreg-
nable against the assault of the Mylin
machine which had defeated several of
Lehigh's opponents on Saturday after-
noons when the opposition was suf-
fering from attacks of over-confidence
because of upsets the previous week.

A poor punt by Steve Smoke, rookie
halfback who has shown that, with
experience and a vast amount of additional knowledge, he may be the
spearhead of the Lehigh attack in the
next two years, set the stage for the
sole Lafayette tally of the day. The
try for extra point was low and wide.

Realizing that ground could not be
gained against the line charges of the
Engineers, the Lafayette team decided
to defend its score from then on.
Punts were exchanged on first downs
throughout the game as Smoke chal-
lenged Moyer for distance.

A total of 45 punts, the majority of
them traveling considerable distances
under adverse weather conditions, re-

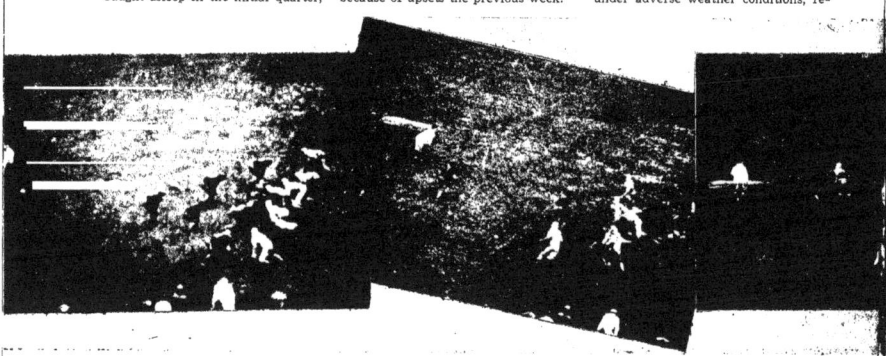

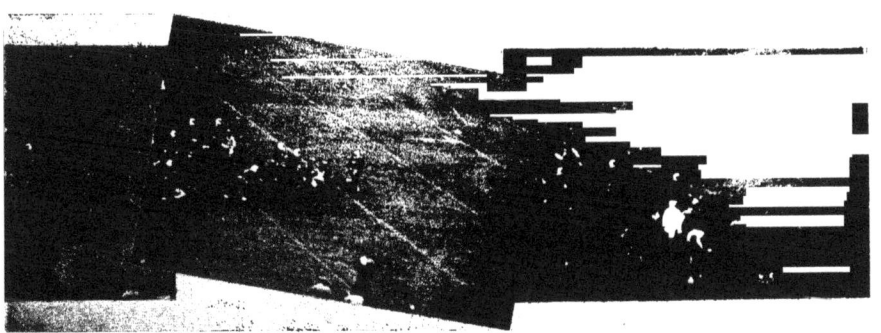

Lehigh, 0

By
CHARLES MORAVEC
Asst. University News Editor

vealed that the Brown and White sophomore gained a total of 1,135 yards (over half a mile) against 966 by Moyer.

That yardage was gained after the scoring was all over was by the Engineers who outplayed the Leopards through the second half and handed them a scare by driving to the 9-yard line where the ball was lost on downs after an attempted pass was missed by Melloy. Other than the 32-yard gallop to the goal line by Moyer, the Leopards gained a total of 37 yards as compared to 72 by the Engineers.

Lehigh rooters were on the edge of their seats late in the second quarter when Moyer fumbled deep in Maroon territory and three Engineers attempted to recover only to miss out in favor of Stellatella.

When all statistics are tallied, the battle of the neighborly rivalry that originated before the turn of the century was fought by two anxious elevens. But for each combination, it was a sophomore that carried the burden on defense and around Smoke of Lehigh and Moyer of Lafayette the game revolved.

Muhlenberg, 20; Lehigh, 0

Capitalizing on two definite breaks, the Muhlenberg College football team, enjoying one of its best seasons during the past ten years, came to Taylor Field to defeat the Engineers, 20-0 in the 28th game of the series.

Both Lehigh and Muhlenberg teams battled on even terms throughout the first quarter with the Engineers showing a fundamental offense which carried them into Mules' territory. Early in the second quarter, Melvin Paul broke through the Engineers line to grab the ball as Cox attempted to pass to Smoke on a reverse play and raced 45 yards for the first score of the day. Franklin converted the extra point from placement.

The second touchdown was the result of a 91-yard drive started in the third period when Stamus ran back one of Smoke's punts for 29 yards to his own 38. Using power plays, Stamus, Brundzo, and Burin carried the ball to the Engineers' 4 yard stripe where Burin skirted around left end for a

Typical of the second half was this Lehigh aggressiveness. Moyer of Lafayette attempts a run from a kick position, is rushed by the Lehigh line and finally tackled for a 10 yd. loss on the Lafayette 14 yd. line. The game was played in a sea of mud.

Lehigh's Smoke takes the ball on the Lafayette 35 yd. line . . .

touchdown. Brundzo's attempted placement was blocked.

As the Engineers threatened in the final period, Reichwein intercepted a pass from Cox intended for Simpson and thrilled a crowd of close to 7,000 spectators as he ran 95 yards for a touchdown. Dawe's placement ended the scoring with the score 20-0.

N. Y. U., 45; Lehigh, 0

Seven Violet players from New York University, tired of three successive defeats, shared the scoring honors when the Engineers travelled to Ohio Field on Nov. 5 for the 11th game of the existing rivalry.

Dr. Mal Stevens' boys accounted for two touchdowns in the opening quarter, another in the second, two more in the third, and another pair in the final quarter as the Brown and White squad was completely outclassed and outplayed.

The Violet scores were made by rushes and a sharp and accurate aerial attack. Stan Mikulka, Danny Dowd, Dill Galu, Orlando Ciraco, Woody Wittekind, Joe LaManna, and Art Schillig each scored once while Campanis, Galu, and LaManna made good for three extra points.

Harmeson's charges never threatened until the final minutes of the ball game when they accumulated three first downs out of four they gained all afternoon. All of these were scored on passes thrown by Wertz and Cox.

The Engineers were stopped every time they were ready to try something different, and could do nothing about the Violets' maneuvers except ground a few passes.

It was the Violets' second straight victory over the Engineers and the largest score they tallied all season.

Season's Statistics

Registering a total of 61 first downs this season, the Engineers gained 1842 yards by rushes and forward passes which enabled an inexperienced backfield to score a total of 60 points during the season.

Statistics reveal that the Engineers were penalized 31 times for a total of 207 yards lost. In addition, the Brown and White gridders failed to recover nine fumbles throughout the nine games.

All of the scores were made by sophomores and juniors who saw little or no action last season. Dick Gowdy, substitute halfback, scored three times for a total of 18 points. Alfred Cox, who completed his third year of football for his entire high school and college career, was second with 12 points. Herb Feucht, Charles Conover, George Melloy, and Steve Smoke each scored six points. Duyckinck, who brought the margin of victory to the Engineers in the first game of the season against Pennsylvania Military College, had a total of four points. Charles Griffiths and Emery Loomis each have one point to their credit by virtue of extra points after touchdown.

Cox was the leading ground gainer

follows his interference toward right tackle . . .

finds an opening and plunges through the line . . .

meets the Lafayette secondary at the 28 yd. mark . . .

and pushes on to the 25 yd. line before being tackled.

during the season. He reeled off 409 yards by rushing and passing. In addition, Cox completed eight out of thirty-four passes for a total of 113 yards.

Smoke averaged 40 yards for 78 kicks and was the second highest ground gainer with a total of 407 yards to his credit.

Forty-eight contests have been scheduled for Lehigh athletes in basketball, swimming, and wrestling for the winter months. In addition, the Engineers will stage two prep school meets and act as hosts for the Eastern Intercollegiate Swimming Association championships at Taylor gymnasium.

Varsity Basketball

Dec. 9—Upsala ....home
Dec. 14—Syracuse ....home
Dec. 17—Wittenberg ....home
Jan. 13—Alfred ....home
Jan. 17—Muhlenberg ....home

Feb. 3—Gettysburg ....home
Feb. 8—Haverford ....home
Feb. 11—Swarthmore ....home
Feb. 15—Bucknell ....home
Feb. 18—Villanova ....home
Feb. 22—Rutgers ....away
Feb. 25—Lafayette ....home
Feb. 27—Muhlenberg ....away
March 1—Rutgers ....away
March 4—Lafayette ....away

Freshman Basketball

Jan. 14—Hun School ....home
Feb. 11—Freeland M. & M. ....home
Feb. 17—Wyoming Seminary ....home
Feb. 18—Perkiomen Prep ....home
Feb. 22—Rutgers '42 ....away
Feb. 25—Lafayette '42 ....home
March 1—Rutgers '42 ....home
March 4—Lafayette '42 ....away

Varsity Swimming

Jan. 7—Princeton ....away
Jan. 14—Pennsylvania ....away
Feb. 11—Rutgers ....away
Feb. 18—Delaware ....home
Feb. 25—Johns Hopkins ....away
March 4—Swarthmore ....away

March 11—Eastern Intercollegiates .....home

Freshman Swimming

Feb. 4—Blair Academy ....away
Feb. 11—Rutgers '42 ....away
March 1—Lafayette '42 ....home
March 4—Mercersburg Academy ......away

Varsity Wrestling

Jan. 11—Nebraska ....home
Jan. 14—Cornell ....home
Feb. 4—Navy ....away
Feb. 11—Penn State ....away
Feb. 15—Yale ....away
Feb. 18—Syracuse ....home
Feb. 25—Princeton ....away
Feb. 28—Lafayette ....home
March 4—V. M. I. ....home
March 10 & 11—Eastern Intercollegiates .....away

Freshman Wrestling

Feb. 18—Mercersburg Academy ......away
Feb. 21—Wyoming Seminary ....home
Feb. 28—Lafayette '42 ....home
March 1—Princeton '42 ....away
March 4—Pennsylvania '42 ....home

Tournaments

Feb. 4—7th Annual Prep School Swimming Tournament ....home
March 3 & 4—4th Annual Prep School Wrestling Tournament ....home

Letters to the Editor

(Continued from page one)

high standards, and many of them have consistently good football teams. Some time ago a graduate of Lehigh said to me that he did not see why a lot of husky boys could learn calculus, but seem utterly unable to learn the intricacies of football. This might bring up the question of coaching, but I agree with others that you mentioned in your article, in that I do not think the fault lies with the coaching.

I agree heartily with some kind of an investigation, while I do not like that word, but something that will satisfy the Alumni, as it is very evident thre is something wrong somewhere. We all know to what extent the Yale or Princeton alumni become aroused simply when they do not have winning teams. I do not think the Lehigh Alumni strive for always having winning teams, but I am sure, every loyal son of Lehigh would like to see a little more consistency in that regard. Perhaps there is generally over-emphasis on college football, and there are abuses that should be corrected, but sport is a great thing and has millions of lovers in this world, but those teachers and alumni who feel there is no room for it simply do not possess human instincts, which to my mind are quite as essential as an overly lot of learning to fit the youth for his life after leaving college.

With kind regards, I am
Sincerely yours,
CLASS OF '02·

Alumni Committee

My Dear Mr. Parsons:—

First, permit me to congratulate you for opening up the question of "Football Policy." It has been the most talked of subject among the Lehigh Alumni and at the same time a subject which no one has, in the past, presented in printing of discussed at any official Alumni Meeting.

I assume this letter will be but a drop in the torrent that you receive and that just as many different opinions are expressed as snow flakes in a blizzard.

My suggestion is the appointment of an Alumni Committee to interview Alumni of other colleges who are in Lehigh's class and develop, if possible, how they handle their problems. This committee to make a report and recommendations for action at the June Alumni Meeting.

My further suggestion is to make haste slowly but surely and surely. I believe the Lehigh situation can be improved.

Anything that the writer can do to co-operate, will be gladly done
Very truly yours,
CLASS OF '11·

"All Within My Power"

Dear Mr. Parsons:

As one of the younger graduates of Lehigh I wish to say that your article of the November issue of the BULLETIN was indeed a far-reaching word for one of Lehigh's direct needs.

I have the same sentiments as you have expressed in your article, and most definitely feel that Lehigh is in the position to have a football team commensurate with the University scholastic reputation.

You may be sure that I will do all within my power to help your policy and if there is work to be done that I will be the first to volunteer. Certainly we have been "razzed" long enough about our football teams and I hope the day will come, through your efforts and mine that we may raise our heads to an "all-around" university.

Sincerely yours,
CLASS OF '36·

Pleasant and Unpleasant

Dear Mr. Parsons:

Thank you for your letter of the 22nd inst. in regard to the football situation at Lehigh. Since writing you I have had the pleasant and unpleasant experience of seeing another Lafayette game—pleasant in that the Lehigh team greatly outplayed Lafayette and unpleasant because of the adverse score and the weather.

I make frequent visits to New York and on one of these occasions I hope to have the pleasure of discussing this matter with you—for inasmuch as I now have a freshman son at Lehigh I have an added interest.

Sincerely yours,
CLASS OF '09·

Not a Misdemeanor

Dear Mr. Parsons:

When I read your article in last month's BULLETIN requesting letters from the alumni on the football situation at Lehigh, it occurred to me that it might be just another one of those things. However, your recent article in this month's issue again requests such letters and, inasmuch as you have asked for it twice, you can have it.

It so happens that while I was in college it wasn't necessary to lift our hats to very many people because we had not only winning football teams but were at the top of the heap in all of the sports with the possible exception of track. Certainly anyone who is in his right mind would not like to revert to the athletic conditions of that period.

However, I could not feel that it is a misdemeanor to capitalize on one's athletic ability and I believe that Lehigh has gone from the ridiculous to the sublime in reference to its athletics. By that I mean that when I was in college the athletic situation was notorious from the standpoint of paid athletes and while we had winning teams in practically every branch of sports, it certainly wasn't conducive to the man with natural athletic ability to compete for a position on the football or baseball teams where the paid athletes were naturally receiving preference on the positions.

At the present time it appears to me that if a man has athletic ability and desires to receive a scholarship or help from the University that almost every obstacle possible is thrown in his way.

I make such a statement because during the past 15 years I have been contacted by a number of individuals who desire to receive an education. It is impossible for their families to procure such education for them because of circumstances. They are boys of a very high type, good scholars, and natural athletes and it would seem to me that providing such a person with the necessary requisites to receive an education is entirely in line with good ethics.

Several paragraphs in your article have struck pretty close to home. It so happens that I have two boys whom I hope will enroll at Lehigh. As a matter of fact, the older one, just entering high school at the present time, has evinced a desire to enroll at Lehigh and study chemical engineering. I have noticed recently that the other boys in the crowd have ridiculed such a desire, not only to my son but, in a joking way, to me. I am hopeful that such ridicule can be laughed off but a boy at the age of 13 is rather of an impressionable mind and certainly somebody has a job to do to keep him in line with his ideas at the present time.

One of the things that particularly disgusted me about the athletic situation at Lehigh was the abolishment of Lacrosse as a major sport. Certainly somebody showed poor judgment in such a decision even though the sport was not self-sustaining. There were very few years in the entire history of the sport at Lehigh that the Lacrosse team did not secure some kind of a championship, either divisional or intercollegiate and it was at least one sport where the amateur had a real chance to make good before his graduation. It is most embarrassing to those who were connected with that sport at Lehigh to see the present mediocre or might I say incompetent teams representing the University. If the decision is to stand, it would seem to me that it should be eliminated entirely and not permit a group to call themselves a club and represent the University.

All of the foregoing may sound somewhat bitter and perhaps it is but it is at least an expression of opinion and that is what you asked for.

I do not claim to have a solution of the situation but I do feel that the matter of athletic scholarships or aid to athletes, providing they are of the right type and can meet the scholarship requirements of the University should have the restrictions taken off and some effort made to build up the various teams representing the school in athletic competition. Either that or cut them out altogether.

I shall be glad to discuss this situation with you at your convenience.

CLASS OF '17·

Prexy's Pen

demic learning, psychology, philosophy, and the record-ed thoughts, feelings and aspirations of mankind as embodied in the literature and arts, contribute to its cultivation. Facility in languages aids in all of these fields. Obviously, attainment in all of these branches of learning transcends the possibilities of a four year college course, which is everywhere found insufficient for mastery of even one of them.

One cult holds a study of political and other social institutions to be a prime requisite in the preparation for citizenship, although there is no evidence that those most familiar with legal and political procedures and customs are the most useful citizens. The major cleav-ages of policy, conservatism, radicalism, nationalism, pacifism, free individualism, communism, and the other *isms*, are determined by general considerations of moral purposes rather than by a knowledge of details of any branch of learning. Private service to society is as meri-torious manifestation of good citizenship as is public service. Hence, it is my conviction that preparation to do competently and honestly whatever one undertakes to do for society is the first requisite of good citizenship. Following close after this is the ability and will to live wholesomely and helpfully in one's immediate neigh-borhood. For example, ignorance and indifference con-cerning infectious diseases and sanitation might permit a voter to do more harm than would be offset by any erudition on the theories of government with which his ballot might be surcharged. Only one universal qualifi-cation for citizenship need be emphasized, therefore, to those who pass through college gates and that is a *sense of civic duty*, since good citizenship results more from motives and integrity than from knowledge in the college bred.

We may assume, therefore, that preparation for citi-zenship can be clustered about any good college course, aimed at developing power of thought, since the basis for civic arts must be gleaned from reading and obser-vation subsequent to graduation in any event. Motivated by a sense of civic honor and responsibilty, any college trained man or woman can participate in the procedures of republican or representative government at a level far above the highest level that American democracy has yet been able to attain. The lives and leadership of Lehigh's alumni, whose preparation has been largely aimed at intelligent participation in the economic and scientific affairs of the world, attest the validity of this thesis.

Much of the discussion about special college prepara-tion for citizenship is, therefore, misleading, since there is no specific body of subject matter which preeminently constitutes a basis for such preparation, and general intelligence with good judgment can be founded on one college curriculum as well as another, assuming a com-mon acquaintaince with elemetary civics afforded by preparatory schooling. Modern social organization in its complexity is served best by the effective cooperation of specialists who have a sense of social and civic respon-sibility coupled with a general intelligence and a will to cooperate. Lehigh prepares men to fulfill such obli-gations of citizenship.

C. C. Williams

UCH discussion goes on nowadays about educa-tion for citizenship,—presumably acquainting students with such matters as will enable them to vote intelligently and to perform such other du-ties as may pertain to their connection with demo-cratic government. Inquiries frequently come to me anent the policy at Lehigh on this point. The views most commonly expressed tacitly assume that effective citi-zenship is manifested solely or chiefly in the individual's very small share of influence in running the government rather than in performing the duties of daily life which constitute his own private career and, by the same token, his vital contribution non-politically to the social and economic fabric of his country. Some assume also that there is a certain body of academic subject matter which is peculiarly appropriate as preparation for citizenship, while others conceive a so-called "integrated personal-ity," an all-round or universal man, who is prepared at all points and ready for any eventuality.

To vote and perform other civic duties intelligently involves judgment concerning much more than a know-ledge of governmental machinery and procedures, which for the most part have been rather arbitrarily adopted and vary from time to time and place to place. Under-standing the elements which comprise the social and economic *milieu* and the forces which fuse these elements into a social organization and having a vital part in that organization worthy to be represented, are more impor-tant as the bases of political judgment than is a familiar-ity with political instrumentalities.

So far as I have observed, no one branch or group of academic subjects is superior to all others for conferring understanding and sound judgment in matters pertaining to public policy in the aggregate, although specialists may excel in discernment at particular points. One finds individuals in any one of a great diversity of educated groups well informed and judicious about public affairs while at the same time other representatives of these same groups are ill-informed and erratic. Certainly no one group has produced unanimously a convincingly clear and sound exposition of the complicated problems which especially vex us at present. History and a' fam-iliarity with economic and social institutions form a good background; a knowledge of natural, biologic and phy-sical sciences, particularly in their applied forms, is especially advantageous in this "scientific age"; an un-derstanding of human nature is important. The latter is largely intuitive, but insofar as it derives from aca-

16

The Directors Look Ahead

(Continued from page eleven)

entered college. He wound up by saying he hoped Homecoming Day, so successfully inaugurated, would continue for many years to come.

Robert Farnham, '99 asked the Executive Secretary to submit his report. During this academic year, dinners and smokers have been held by the following clubs: The Home Club, Central Pennsylvania, Delaware, Detroit, New York, Northern New Jersey, Northeast Pennsylvania, Northern Ohio, Philadelphia, Central Jersey and Western New York. The Pittsburgh, Delaware and Philadelphia Clubs also hold regular weekly luncheons. President Williams is cooperating very nicely with the Alumni Association by having faculty members notify the Association when they plan to go out of town and in this way the clubs are able to capitalize on their presence and arrange for meetings, etc., to hear first-hand news from the campus.

W. H. Lesser, '05 was called on to report on Placement. He stated that 83.1 percent of the class of '38 is now placed in positions, which is an exceedingly high record as compared with other colleges. The plan of having Placement Committees in each of the Lehigh Clubs, which was suggested at the Friday afternoon conference last June, is being carried out and so far the New York, Philadelphia and Northeast Pennsylvania clubs have such committees and are trying to help Lehigh men in their respective districts find positions. Although it is quite difficult at this time to place anybody in a job, he believed Lehigh graduates have a wonderful chance and asked the help of everyone in this important matter of placing our men.

Robert Herrick reported for Morton Sultzer, '12, on the New York Club group singing contest. He said the matter was well under way and that the Club had authorized the purchase of a cup to be used as a prize. The rules of the contest are being worked up and there is every indication of its being put into action in spring. The idea is

that these groups of boys from fraternities and dormitories will sing out of doors and it is believed it will attract the townspeople as well as the student body, and will help a lot in making Lehigh the singing college it should be.

Under Undergraduate Contact, A. E. Buchanan, Jr., '18 reported that through the very efficient aid of Dr. Beardslee, a member of his committee, he was very tactfully working up interest among the members of this year's graduating class to carry out a similar insurance plan as undertaken by a number of the class of '38. He believed that even a larger percentage of the class of '39 will participate in this plan.

Caleb Kenney, '10, gave a verbal report on Alumni Day matters. He stated that the Executive Secretary had suggested that at the alumni dinner in June extra-curricular activities be emphasized and that the speakers for the dinner represent this phase of college life. He said the dinner last June, at which the three Deans gave talks, was so fine that we should not have any kind of let-down and we should be mighty careful in planning this year's dinner. The Executive Secretary stated his idea was that we might get as speakers Bosey Reiter, Billy Sheridan and one other; that the alumni always want to see and hear these men and he believed we could work up a mighty attractive program. Kenney said he thought we were right last year in setting up no tables in the gallery at the hotel. The previous year a large number of alumni had seats in the gallery rather than on the main floor. This year again, he suggests we do no provide tables in the gallery but reserve this space more for the wives of alumni to congregate and listen to the program. Kenney also said he thought tables should be provided for groups other than the five year reunion classes; that many came back who were not celebrating a regular reunion and seemed a little at a loss as to where they should sit. This Alumni Day Committee is a new feature and

we are satisfied that the Alumni Association will get a lot of help and suggestions from it.

All of the above standing committee reports were ordered received and filed.

Under new business, all agreed that the Friday afternoon meeting, previous to Alumni Day in June, should be continued, as the discussions seemed to be well worthwhile.

The sentiment of the Board seemed to be that some specific object for raising funds be brought up at the next meeting, but that it was too far in advance to know what the project might be or even whether there should be a project, depending on conditions at the time.

H. D. Wilson's proposal, relative to reading the names of those who had died during the past year at the Alumni Meeting, was discussed. Wilson feels that the sounding of taps and standing in silence is a poor substitute and that the names should be read to pay proper tribute to these men. The concensus of opinion seemed to be that this list is already quite long, would become larger as years go by and that the plan now in practice is all right.

The Executive Secretary stated that the Addressograph machine in the Alumni Office had been giving considerable trouble; that a new machine would cost $495 and that we would receive a small allowance on the old one. It was moved and carried unanimously that the Secretary go ahead with the purchase of a new Addressograph machine.

A brief discussion was held on the athletic situation at Lehigh and President Parsons stated he had received a resolution on the situation from the Northern New Jersey Lehigh Club in addition to many letters from alumni. He assured those present that he personally would keep after the matter.

By motion, at 12:15, the meeting adjourned.

Respectfully submitted,
Wm. A. Cornelius,
Secretary.

The Life of Asa Packer

(Continued from page seven)

developed into the famed Switch-back Railroad of Mauch Chunk which for many years thrilled tourists to the Switzerland of America, with a trip through the clouds at the dizzy speed of 16 miles per hour.

At this time there were in operation in the United States several other short roads of rail of a mile or two in length the rails being of wood, over which cars were drawn by horses or mules; but at the time of its construction in 1827, this railroad, nine miles in length, with cars drawn by mules, was the largest and most important railroad in the country. The Stourbridge Lion, the

first steam locomotive to draw a train in the United States did not make its three-mile trial run on the Delaware and Hudson track until two years later, in 1829. By 1833, the year Asa Packer came down to Mauch Chunk, there had been a few other railroads constructed in the Lehigh Valley and surrounding region, some operated by steam locomotives, but they were used chiefly as feeders for transporting coal to the canals, which were now flourishing. In this year the Delaware and Hudson Canal transported 110,000 tons of coal, the Morris Canal 136,000 tons, the Lehigh Canal 123,000 tons, and the

other canals corresponding amounts.

In Mauch Chunk, Asa Packer at once found employment at his trade, as carpenter in the construction of canal boats. (He had done some winter canal boat construction in the north, at Tunkhannock.) He soon chartered a boat of his own and, doing all the manual labor himself, undertook a traffic between Mauch Chunk and Philadelphia. Successful in this, he secured a second boat. His rapidly expanding business led him to form a partnership with his brother under the title of A. & R. W. Packer.

(To be continued)

17

Northern New York

The Lehigh Club of Northern New York held a dinner meeting at Gold's Delicatessen & Restaurant in Schenectady on Saturday evening, Dec. 3, 1938. Beer was served at 6:00 with a baked ham dinner at 7:00. Eighteen members were present, and four guests —Billy Cornelius, '89, Executive Secretary of the Alumni Association; his oldest son, Bill Cornelius of Kenyon College; Bosey Reiter, of the University's Physical Education Department; and Vance Miller, Dartmouth, '37. The class of '37 took first place in attendance with five members present.

Following the dinner, the meeting was called to order by President J. C. Ryan, '01. Silent tribute was paid to A. D. Badgely, '96, and F. J. Smith, '34, both of whom had passed on since our last meeting. The minutes of the last meeting were read by Secretary N. Y. Coxe, '34, and approved. President Ryan extended his welcome to the two Corneliuses and Bosey, who had come up from Bethlehem as a result of the efforts of W. S. Miller, '34.

A discussion followed concerning several points of interest at the University, namely the policy of retiring the older instructors, the limitation on the number of students enrolled, and the present Athletic Policy. Billy and Bosey both threw considerable light on all three of the topics. In connection with discussion on the Athletic Policy, a resolution passed by the Northern New Jersey Lehigh Club was read. Rather than adopt this resolution, it was decided to draft one of our own to be forwarded to F. W. Parsons, '02, President of the Alumni Association. The matter of a Placement Committee for this district was discussed, and the President appointed the following to serve on this committee: R. W. Wieseman, '16 and N. Y. Coxe, '34 for Schenectady; J. L. Mosher, '10 and M. O. Jefferson, '22 for Albany; and E. J. Decker, '23 for Troy.

The following officers were unanimously elected for the coming year; President, R. W. Wieseman, '16; Secretary, N. Y. Coxe, '34; Treasurer, C. C. Leader, '29. The meeting was then given over to Billy and Bosey, both of whom gave extremely interesting talks. As usual, Bosey's was full of pep and inspiration, and included a poem here and there. Following some interesting movies of several of this year's football games, shown by Billy's son, the meeting was closed with the singing of the Alma Mater, led by Bosey with Charley Leader at the piano.

N. Y. Coxe, '34, Secretary

Northeast Pennsylvania

Football with a capital "F" was the subject of intense discussion at the Hotel Mallow-Sterling in Wilkes-Barre on the evening of November 16 when about 35 members of the Northeastern Pennsylvania Lehigh Club met for their fall banquet.

Speakers from Bethlehem included Paul Short, the new assistant director of athletics; Billy Sheridan, coach of the wrestling team; Wm. A. Cornelius and BULLETIN editor Robert Herrick.

Paul Short, who began a career as a speaker before Lehigh clubs at this meeting, gave an interesting explanation of Lehigh's athletic picture, and showed a remarkable knowledge of the team by analyzing its personnel man for man. He pointed out the handicaps under which the Lehigh teams must work in facing superior opposition that is usually afforded by the teams they play.

Billy Sheridan, the following speaker, seconded many of Short's statements and went on to give a picture of the wrestling team as he expects it to appear in the season which is about to open. He explained that the introduction of wrestling as an extra curricular sport in an increasingly large number of high schools had made it possible to get a higher grade of material in the eastern district, although, of course, this move is of advantage to all colleges with Lehigh trying hard to interest the better boys in its own team.

Mr. Cornelius expressed his pleasure at getting around to these Lehigh dinners where he had an opportunity to meet the alumni who do not get to Bethlehem so often. He called attention to the large enrollment at the University this year and said that the student body is now just about as large as can be accomodated by the present facilities. He further stated that he hoped that as many as possibly could would get down to the Lehigh-Lafayette Game although it was being played at

Buffalo alumni enjoy "broadcast" of Lehigh-Lafayette game.

Lehig

Left, Northern New Jersey alumni pay close attention to speakers on athletic policy. Center, this spirited gathering was photographed prior to the Philadelphia Club's football dinner at Bookbinder's Restaurant.

Clubs

paganda being trained into the Youth of these various nations.

Profesor C. J. Ratzloff, head of the department of economics at Lafayette College was the second speaker and dealt with the future economic and sociological problems which America must face.

The third speaker was Professor Earl Reed Silvers, director of public relations of Rutgers University who talked on the pleasures and pitfalls of short-story writing.

Easton. Unquestionably the team would put up a hard fight.

The meeting was concluded with motion pictures of the Case and P. M. C. Games.

Northern New Jersey

The annual pre-Lafayette game get together of the Northern New Jersey Lehigh Club was held November 15, 1938 at the Suburban Golf Club in Union, New Jersey.

Fifty members and guests were present.

The meeting was opened by H. F. Casselman '32 who was replaced by Robert L. Trainer, '26 as president, after election of officers. Gilbert King '31 was elected vice-president; Lewis Roberts '35 treasurer; Richard Roll '32 sergeant-at-arms; and Arthur H. Loux '35 was reelected secretary.

Introduced in order were our guests from the University, Billy Cornelius, Paul Calvert, Dean Congdon, who presented the inside 'info' on the jitterbug congregation at the jam session held in the hotel, house-party week end, Bob Herrick apologizing for not having the scheduled game films, and the guest of honor, Bosey Reiter.

After Bosey's remarks a lively discussion of the University's football policy ensued and a resolution was passed unanimously. Copies of the resolution have been sent all Lehigh clubs for consideration and it is hoped that next June a meeting will be held with the trustees of the University at which time suitable action may be taken.

A. H. Loux '35, Secretary.

Trenton

With over a hundred in attendance the annual Middle Three Meeting of the Lehigh-Lafayette and Rutgers Clubs was held on the evening of November 14 at the Trenton Club with the genial Pop Pennington presiding over the Lehigh share of the program. The meeting was opened with a talk by Dr. Benjamin L. Miller, head of the department of geology at Lehigh, who described the the stress that is being laid upon Youth in Gemany, Russia and Japan, countries which he recently visited in the course of a world tour. Dr. Miller also reviewed the educational decline in these countries and drew a parallel among them as to pro-

Philadelphia

Philadelphia's annual football dinner, in spite of its new location, went off with an audible bang this year as gridiron minded enthusiasts gathered at the New Bookbinder's Restaurant for their annual discussion and pep rally prior to the Lafayette game.

In probably one of the most serious sessions that Club members have ever experienced, the football problems and policies of Lehigh were brought into the open. This was prefaced by the usual clam and lobster dinner which was enjoyed with the usual air of enthusiasm which surrounds a Lafayette pep rally.

Speakers of the evening were the beloved Bosey Reiter; Glen Harmeson, football coach; Pat Pazzetti, All-American star of '13; and G. R. (Buckie) Macdonald, president of the New York Lehigh Club. R. Dexter Warriner, president of the Philadelphia Club acted as toastmaster and the usual cheers were led capably by Johnny Opdycke.

Interested in the deeper aspects of the football policy at Lehigh as introduced by the Association president, Floyd Parsons, in the ALUMNI BULLETIN, members centered their discussion around the possibility of finding a sane solution to a better football team at their Alma Mater. Phases of the situation much as introduced by Mr. Parsons in his article, were considered by club members and while no resolutions were drawn up, alumni were urged to contact Mr. Parsons, giving him their personal views in the matter.

Announcement was made of the next Philadelphia dinner which is to be held on January 27 at the Bellevue-Stratford.

Center, John Lloyd, president and Bill Lesser, secretary of Northeast Pennsylvania Club. Below, new officers of Northern New Jersey; Trainer, King, Roll, Loux and Roberts. Right, part view of Wilkes-Barre meeting.

BRINGING YOU---

Up to Date

by WALTER R. OKESON
Treasurer, Lehigh University

It appears to be necessary to write an article for almost every issue of the BULLETIN in order to keep you advised of the latest endowment gifts and bequests. Not that this duty irks me—far from it. It is a most joyous task.

Back in the so-called "Gay Nineties" a serious minded young man got his Mechanical Engineering degree at Lehigh. His name was Frank W. Roller and his class was '94. In the October BULLETIN you may have seen his obituary and noted that he died on August 20, 1938. As he had never evinced great interest in his Alma Mater, I was somewhat surprised to receive, a short time ago, a communication from his executors stating that Lehigh was named as a legatee under his will. On reading the will I found that after certain specific bequests, a trust was created under which two persons were given monthly incomes during their lives and upon their deaths the trust terminated and the corpus of the trust was divided 25 percent to Lehigh University, 25 percent to the Orange Memorial Hospital of East Orange, N. J., 25 percent to the Welfare Federation of the Oranges and the balance to individuals.

Create Many Problems

Now just to show that these various legacies create problems which keep the Treasurer's life from being all "beer and skittles", I might mention that already suit has been brought to have the probate of this will set aside, the petitioner alleging incapacity and undue influence. Of course, Lehigh must defend her interests and this adds a lawyer in New Jersey to Lehigh's list of counsel which includes attorneys in Bethlehem, Philadelphia, New York, Wilkes-Barre and Washington. Almost every large bequest brings with it some legal problem to be settled in court or by negotiation. Perhaps the strangest suit was one we joined in a short time ago to show that the testator's instructions to his executors to spend $250,000 on a mausoleum diverted to this purpose an unreasonably large proportion of his estate. The Court reduced this amount to $100,000 thus adding to the residual estate $150,000.00.

Another case which we settled out of Court concerned a post-nuptial agreement which deprived a surviving husband of any legal rights to a share in his wife's estate. As she was much younger than her husband, her will was evidently drawn with the idea that he would predecease her and he

was left with only small life interest. Feeling that she would wish him properly provided for, Lehigh agreed to make this provision, giving him a reasonable monthly income.

Consider True Desires

In this connection I might say that in every case of surviving family members, Lehigh's trustees always consider what the testator would probably desire and act accordingly even though it is against Lehigh's interest. Their feeling is that no advantage should be taken of a benefactor's generosity and in settling any question the welfare of the testator's survivors is first considered.

A few weeks ago an alumnus of my own age and vintage dropped in to see me. He was writing a new will and he had provided for a legacy of $10,000 for Lehigh but he was anxious to make this $50,000 if he could be assured two things were possible. One was that the income from this amount could go to some relatives during their lifetime and the other was that Lehigh would accept this legacy and agree to act as trustee for the life tenants. I assured him that legacies creating life tenants with Lehigh as residual legatee were most usual and, while not so usual, we did accept gifts or legacies in trust insofar as concerned one or more life tenants. His mind relieved on these points, he stated that I would shortly receive a copy of this clause in his will.

Two weeks later another alumnus handed me $50,000 of stock as an outright gift with the proviso that during his lifetime we pay the net income, whatever it might be, to certain relatives. The stock is ours to do with as we please. We can sell it and reinvest the proceeds as we can in the case of any other of our endowment securities. We are obligated to pay only any net income received during the donor's lifetime to the beneficiaries named by him. He, of course, must pay a gift tax on the basis of the estimated present value of this income. He pays no tax on the prinicipal as it is a gift to an educational institution and, in fact, up to 15 percent of his personal income, he can use this gift to reduce his income tax.

So since my article was written for the October BULLETIN several hundred thousand dollars has been added towards that goal of a $15,000,000 endowment which we all hope to see Lehigh reach within a reasonable number of years.

Engineer---The
(Continued from page one)

engineering profession to take all of his time. His family life and recreation have proved an enjoyable outlet for his boundless activities. In 1906 he was married to the daughter of Bishop Talbot, for years a trustee of Lehigh University The Donaldsons now live in West Chester County with their three children.

Only recently this Lehigh man toured Northern Europe on a bicycle and finds recreation in outdoor activities such as skiing, skating, fishing and tennis. As vice-president of the Mason and Hanger Company and of Silas Mason Company, Inc., he is an outstanding man in his field. Here he gives you his picture of the new Lincoln Tunnel project as he sees it.

In 1927 the Mason & Hanger Company, which with its predecessors had been building things for a century, adopted a new slogan and went to work with fresh vigor. The slogan, although never written and seldom expressed, was "Deep, Difficult and Dangerous."

The first job undertaken was the foundations for the West Tower of the George Washington Bridge—open cofferdams of unprecedented depth in the Hudson River silt—and the Fulton-Cranberry Street Subway Tunnel under the East River to Brooklyn. The subway job comprised two eighteen foot tubes, each one and one-half miles long, running from Church Street, Manhattan, through Fulton Street to the East River, and then under Brooklyn Heights to a point beyond the approaches of the Brooklyn Bridge. Every foot of these tubes was driven under compressed air, reaching a pressure of 40 pounds per square inch under the middle of the East River. The tubes passed beneath three operating subways, beneath several elevated railroads, beneath the massive structure of the Brooklyn Bridge, and on Fulton Street went directly outside of and beneath the foundations of many important buildings, some twenty stories in height. This job—the most difficult of its kind attempted up to that time and perhaps since—served as a good introduction for the company's entrance into the compressed air tunneling business.

Built New Projects

In the next few years the Mason & Hanger Company, with its associated Silas Mason Company, built compressed air tunnels in Philadelphia, a second pair of subway tubes under the East River, and a Vehicular Tunnel beneath Boston Harbor, so that when the first tube of the Lincoln Tunnel was advertised for bids in 1934 it felt itself the logical contractor. This proved to be the case and after the bids were opened it found itself in possession of a $6,400,000.00 contract for

20

Story of Francis Donaldson

constructing a tube thirty-one feet in diameter and a mile long beneath the Hudson River.

The job, as far as surface and subsurface conditions went, was similar to the Holland Tunnel constructed in 1921 except that the tunnel was one and one-half feet bigger in diameter. The contract included but one tube, it being the plan to build the second tube subsequently. The tunnel started from both ends in rock, but the bulkhead lines broke out into the famous Hudson River silt, with which the gorge of the Hudson River is uniformly filled. In New Jersey the change was abrupt, the rock bank of the river sloping steeply to unknown depths, but on the New York side the rock surface rose and fell so that this portion of the tunnel had to be built in that most difficult kind of material known as "mixed face."

Avoid Pressure Joining

The contract required the construction of the tunnel with two shields, the probable intent being to drive a shield from either shore until the two met beneath the river. Our experience in removing the interior framework of heavy shields under high air pressure, a necessity on our East River tunnels, suggested that we should avoid it this time if possible. We therefore planned to drive the New Jersey shield all the way across the river and to terminate its journey in a huge caisson sunk just outside the New York bulkhead line into which it would be possible to seal the lining and thus remove the shield in free air. The New York shield would terminate in the same caisson but, due to its shorter path would get there first in spite of the more difficult material through which it would have to travel and would be removed while the New Jersey shield was still under way.

Work on both sides of the river was commenced simultaneously, the first step being to erect huge air compressor plants including on each side low air compressors with a capacity of 22,000 cu. ft. of free air a minute and high air compressors with a capacity of 4,000 cu. ft., together with the necessary electrical equipment to operate and control them. A large permanent shaft was sunk into rock beneath the New Jersey Palisades and a construction shaft on the easterly end of the job near Eleventh Avenue, New York. At this point it was necessary to drive heavy steel piling to rock to permit the upper part of the shaft to be excavated. At the same time preparations were made for sinking the caisson in New York, which, in addition to its function as a place to dismantle the tunnel shields, was to form the foundation for the New York River ventilation building. The lower part of the caisson was fabricated at the Federal Shipyard in Newark and when the

time was ripe it was towed up the Hudson like a big ship and, with flags flying and whistles tooting, floated into a guide frame made of piles and timber.

The caisson was then sunk to grade under compressed air in the usual way, the walls being built up in lifts as the excavation proceeded. Most of the sinking was done through silt but some eight or ten feet of rock had to be removed before subgrade was reached. It may be noted here that the cost of such rock excavation in the caisson under an air pressure of thirty-five or forty pounds per square inch can be only compared with the cost of the material excavated in a decayed tooth by a high class dentist.

By the time the caisson was sunk and sealed, both the New Jersey and New York shafts had been finished, the shields had been erected, the necessary airlocks installed, and tunneling was in progress. In New York all material within the bore of the tunnel had to be excavated and removed through the lock so progress was relatively slow, it being possible to average only six or seven feet a day.

It may be well to explain that the structure of the tunnel tube consists of successive rings of cast iron segments, bolted together, each ring being erected with the tail of the shield. The plungers of the shield jacks thrust against the last ring. In the Lincoln Tunnel each ring is composed of fourteen segments and a key, all 30 inches wide and bolted together with 145 1¾ inch high tensile steel bolts.

In ground like that on the New York side the excavating cycle consists of cutting from the face of the tunnel a vertical slice equal in length to the width of a lining segment, then pushing the shield ahead and erecting a ring of segments behind the jacks. In sand or gravel it is necessary to prevent the inward collapse of the face by maintaining a tight structure of horizontal boards called breast boards over its entire area. The excavating process consists of beginning at the top and moving these boards forward the length of the shove, one at a time, supporting them by struts to the frame of the shield. After all boards have been moved the system of struts is transferred back through the openings in the shield to girders supported by the completed iron lining behind so that the shield may be shoved, its cutting edge being forced into the ground around the perimeter of the breast boarding. In mixed face the top must be breast boarded to the rock surface, the rock being drilled with numerous short holes and carefully blasted so as to avoid wrecking the breast boarding immediately above. It is easily seen why work of this kind is slow.

In silt, however, the problem is entirely different. The Hudson River

silt, to stick to our dental simile, looks and acts very much like gray toothpaste and it is possible to advance a shield driven tunnel through it without removing any of it at all within the bore. This was actually done in the old Hudson-Manhattan Tubes of 16 ft. diameter. Here the face of the shield was entirely closed and the shield was jacked ahead from the lining, ring by ring, the displaced silt forming a ridge in the bottom of the river similar to that formed on a front lawn by a mole. In the case of a modern vehicular tunnel with a diameter of about thirty-one feet, the volume of silt displaced is too great to permit this to be done and at the same time to keep the shield to grade; experience has shown that it is necessary to admit from one-third to one-half of the displaced material and to let it lie on the bottom of the tube as ballast until shield driving is finished.

The two things which chiefly make for progress in silt are the handling of the admitted material in such a way as not to interfere with the erection and bolting together of the segmental rings, and the rapid bolting of these rings themselves.

In the Holland Tunnel, where all work was performed by hand, the highest month's advance was 555 ft. We devised a conveyor for carrying away silt admitted through hydraulically controlled gates in the face of the shield and a mechanical bolt tightener actuated by compressed air, and attained a maximum advance of 1,040 ft. in a month, driving the New Jersey shield 5,060 ft. across the river to the caisson in seven months. The viscosity of the silt and the closed face of the shield permit much lower air pressure to be carried within the tunnel than that called for by the hydrostatic head outside. This pressure, 16 to 18 pounds per square inch, legally permitted the use of eight-hour shifts but we elected to work the men only six hours at the eight-hour rate of pay, considering that the increased output per man would more than compensate for the increased labor cost. This proved to be the case.

Only Mucking Remained

After shield driving was completed, the lining sealed to the caisson walls, and air pressure removed, there remained the mucking out of the admitted silt and the construction of the permanent concrete lining. The silt was removed by small air driven shovels loading into buckets on flat cars, the material within the pockets formed by the flanges of the segments being mucked by hand. Concrete was placed in a series of six operations, each following behind the other, the form for the ceiling being the last in the procession. In general, each form was 80 ft. long and half of the series was concreted daily, the forms on the other half being moved ahead. A progress of 40 ft. a day was thus attained. The entire contract was completed in about two and one-half years.

Personals

OBITUARIES

W. A. Warren, '79

William Alexander Warren, retired consulting engineer, died in Seattle, Washington, on October 31, 1938, at the age of 83.

Born in Beaver County, Pennsylvania in 1855, he worked for the Northern Pacific railway in construction after leaving the University. In 1883 he left for South America where he worked in Chile for six months, and then went into Argentina where he worked for seven years on irrigation projects and railroad construction.

In 1891 Mr. Warren returned to the United States, and in 1898 went to Alaska and worked on the construction of the Valdez railroad up the Copper river. From 1910 to 1922 he worked in Seattle.

In 1922 Mr. Warren left the United States again, this time for Siberia where he spent ten years on railroad and irrigation work and as a consulting engineer of the great steel plant at Kuznetz.

L. H. Kunkle, '98

The Greensburg, Pa. post-office advises that Lewis Harry Kunkle, is deceased. No details are available.

J. H. Bender, '13

John Harry Bender, '13, prominent dentist of Ashland, Pa., died at his home on July 14, following an illness of six weeks. Uremic poisoning and complications caused his death.

Born in Ashland, Dr. Bender prepared for Lehigh at the Ashland High School and Bethlehem Preparatory School. He received the degree of DDS from the University of Pennsylvania.

He enlisted in the U. S. Army Dental Corps and attained the rank of Captain, and in 1919 he opened his office in Ashland.

He was a member of St. Mauritius Church and of the Holy Name Society of that body. He belonged to the Bernard J. Dolan Post, American Legion, and was a member of the Elks and the Fountain Springs Country Club.

His widow, and one daughter survive him. Three sisters and three brothers also survive.

E. T. Corrigan, '18

Edward Thomas Corrigan, B. A., died on October 20, in Philadelphia. He had been an investigator for the Commonwealth of Pennsylvania for the past six years.

His widow, and one son, Donald, survive him.

R. A. Broome, '26

Ross Alexander Broome, B. S. in Bus. Ad., '26- died November 9 at his home in Quakertown. Shock, resulting from an automobile collision, is believed to have been the cause of death.

Born in Scranton, he graduated from the Scranton Technical High School and then went to Lehigh. He lived in Quakertown for the past eleven years and was a member of the First Evangelical and Reformed Church, secretary of the Kiwanis Club, treasurer of the Young People's Republican Club and was borough auditor for Quakertown.

He was a partner in the Shearer-Broome gas station at the time of his death.

His parents and a maternal grandmother, Mrs. A. D. Stell, survive him.

L. A. DeGroot, '28

Lester A. DeGroot died suddenly in Jamaica Hospital on Friday, October 7.

After leaving Lehigh in 1926, Mr. DeGroot was graduated from the Brooklyn Law School and admitted to the bar in 1932.

He had been receiving treatment for a kidney ailment and suffered from pernicious anemia, but did not become seriously ill until about two days before his death.

Mr. DeGroot was a member of the Alpha Chi Rho Fraternity. His mother, a brother and two sisters survive him.

MARRIAGES

CLASS OF 1910

Lovell Lawrence, Jr., to Miss Betsy Osenga of Midland Park, N. J. in Christ Episcopal Church. Pompton Lakes, N. J. on November 12.

CLASS OF 1932

Allan Ayers to Miss Helen Stokes in Glastonbury, Conn., on November 19.

CLASS OF 1934

E. S. Lloyd to Miss Ruth Gardner Williams. at Wilkes-Barre on October 22.

CLASS OF 1935

Charles W. Lueders, Jr., to Miss Deborah Virginia Wolcott, on June 25 in Wayne, Pa.

CLASS OF 1937

A. B. Bornstein to Miss Ethel Goldberg in Bethlehem on November 6.

Ralph S. Heller to Miss Grace Buchhecker of Bethlehem on November 5.

E. W. Hildebrand to Miss Myra Sheffer on October 23 in Harrisburg.

BIRTHS

CLASS OF 1917

To Mr. and Mrs. Bernard H. Jacobson, a daughter, Emily Gail, on September 15.

CLASS OF 1931

To Rev. and Mrs. Revere Beasley, a son, Alfred Leonard, on October 25.

To Mr. and Mrs. James S. Little, a daughter, on October 9.

To Mr. and Mrs. W. F. McGarrity, a daughter, Jean Eleanor, on August 11.

CLASS OF 1933

To Mr. and Mrs. N. J. Tuttle, a son, on November 11.

CLASS OF 1937

To Mr. and Mrs. Frank Minnich, a son, Charles Franklin, on October 25.

PERSONALS

CLASS OF 1889

George W. Harris, Correspondent
12 Holland Terrace, Montclair, N. J.

A favorite expression of former Henry Watterson, one of Kentucky's most famous editors, runs, "Death lurks on the upper road and Injins on the lower one". Into 'such a peaceful and home-like atmosphere of killers and moonshiners, plunged Arthur Moult Smyth, armed only with a brand-new diploma. Smyth continues in a most interesting account of his wanderings in the rough mining country of the Americas, for a number of years after leaving Old South Mountain's sheltering arms.

From Kentucky, he went to Arizona where he lived and worked with Baron Metschki, a Polish Revolutionary and an outstanding mining expert. In Kentucky and Arizona, Smyth learned many things not given in Textbooks. Our classmate admits that he is "Bugs on reading foreign languages"; he has taught French and Spanish and in his travels, in South America found his linguistic ability quite a valuable asset. He said that he met a lawyer in Rio who read eleven languages besides Portugese; he didn't know how to say a word in any one of them and had only one eye and that crossed. Smyth seems to have gotten bravely over his wanderlust, has a pleasant job with Sharp & Dohme, manufacturing pharmaceutical chemists, in Philadelphia, which together with an absorbing hobby, leaves him no dull moments.

Smyth is fond of Interior Decoration, has perfected a scheme for ceiling work which came out in Popular Science and altogether he is as busy as a one-armed paper hanger. He wrote a fine longhand letter instead of a typewritten one, "due to his typewriting be damnable." His writing has the saving grace of being consistent, which is more than can be said of the English language.

A good word comes in from Ralph Barnard, Frank Carman, Arch Johnston and Frederick Weihe—cheerful news about themselves and encouragement as to their intentions to be present at our 50th.

Ralph Barnard and his wife spent a good part of the summer in Maine and have recently returned from a visit to the Lincolns in Elkhorn, West Virginia. While they were in Elkhorn, they took several rides over the scenic mountains of West Virginia and negotiated all the hairpin turns in that part of the country. On their way home to Washington, the Barnards drove over the new part of the Skyline Drive, right on the top of the Blue Ridge Mountains.

Frank Carman and his wife were greatly benefited by their summer's stay at Atlantic City, for doesn't "the salt breath of the sea bring health," and who can withstand the illusive charm of old ocean? The Carmans are now at their old quarters. 33 Washington Square West, New York City.

Frederick Weihe, in acknowledging your correspondent's letter, adds that a generous reply can be expected—already started—but that he will be obliged to have frequent interruptions depending on the demands of his business. No doubt but what his word is as good as his bond and we will be glad to get further word from him.

Arch Johnston wrote about our coming reunion and hopes that we will be fortunate enough to corral the majority of the '89rs now on "The Good Earth," adding that goodness knows that we will never have another 50th. Those of us who were at Camels Hump during our 35th will never forget how each one loosened up while sitting around an open fire after the banquet. Plans are still in the making about our Golden Anniversary but '89rs' don't need to be reminded that we always have a bang-up time at our reunions. There is a special lure about a 50th.

About the time the December BULLETIN reaches its readers, it will be the glorious Yuletide season and your '89' Press Representative sends his very best wishes for your happiness during the Holiday season.

CLASS OF 1890

H. A. Foering, Correspondent
Bethlehem Trust Bldg., Bethlehem, Pa.

We have a very interesting letter from Cardenas, resident at Managua, Nicaragua. He sends material for the 50 year book of Class of '90-Adolfo has been a very busy man, all his life, and has occupied many high positions in civil and political life in Nicaragua.

Among these have been a few appointments to the United States, as for example, "Second Secretary of the Nicaraguan legation and Engineer-Secretary of the Nicaraguan Boundary Commission, Washington, D. C." "Members of the Nicaraguan Delegation to the Second Pan-American Financial Congress held in Washington."

He was Under-Secretary of Foreign Affairs for Nicaragua in 1922.

At the present time he is a member of the "Technical Faculty of Costa Rica"; also a charter member, and President of "Association General de Ingenieros de Nicaragua."

CLASS OF 1891

Walton Forstall, Correspondent
Ithan Ave., Rosemont, Pa.

J. Z. Miller had an exhibition of his oil paintings in November in the old Buchanan homestead, Wheatland, near Lancaster, Pa., Parker-Smith's notice of Douglas' novel reminds your correspondent that Hillman has recently written "The House-Boat Enigma,' a tale of mystery and romance without the conventional murder. As one has said referring to both Miller and Hillman, "Astonishing what engineers will do in spare and unguarded moments."

Paine will be 70 in January, and in the ordinary course of events, this would mean his retirement as Librarian of the Syracuse Public Library. The Trustees are not willing to part with him, however, and have obtained a two-year extension of service.

Three score and ten is a distinguished age, and the few who attain it deserve honorable

mention. So your correspondent went to the 50-year Book, that monument to the class love and industry of Morris. He found one birthday as early as '60, but they were not frequent 'till '68. He regrets that these anniversaries were not noted at the time. He begins his records with 1938. In the past there are: M. C. Smith, March; Hillman and Merrick, August 15 and 17; Boatrite, September; F. H. Davis and J. R. Davis, both October 26; Beck, November, Patterson, Reets and Rench, December 10, 11 and 12. Fertig will be 70 on January 9, and Paine on January 13. What venerable sages have become the lads of September, 1887!

CLASS OF 1894

I. I. Beinhower, Guest Correspondent
25 N. Main St., Rutland, Vt.

"Heigh-ho, heigh-ho" we are now starting on our way to the 45th Reunion in Bethlehem, June next.

Please check your calendar for June 9 and 10, 1939 to be without fail in Bethlehem for this memorable event. We most earnestly desire to surpass all previous records for a dinner attendance.

Please be sure to get in immediate touch with your most intimate classmates and do your utmost to have them meet you in Bethlehem next June.

It is with the deepest regret that we learn of Dr. Aubrey Weymouth's heart attack several weeks ago, and necessitating his confinement to his home. We sincerely hope that he will soon be out and back in his office. I suggest that you drop him a line to help cheer him up.

The rough old steam roller of time "gave an awful jolt" to William Arthur Payne early this year and he advises that he was out of commission from January 1 to September this year. I am happy to say that he has recovered so as to get back to his office, but must take it easy.

I had lunch and a nice visit with Tommy Wilson a few weeks ago; at the duPont in Wilmington. He is going strong, and as most of us know, Tommy is the Power, Light and Traction magnate of Wilmington. He is the very first to say that he will be on hand June next.

I also had lunch with Jim Burley in New York about two weeks ago and am happy to say that Jim is very well and you all know he is 100 per cent back of the propaganda and program for a record turnout for our 45th reunion.

Kavanaugh, of the sleepy City of Brotherly Love, has come to the front with BULLETIN assistance but he feels rather down-hearted and gloomy over the results on Lehigh athletic fields. Cheer up, "Kavvy" better times are on the way. He advises that he has already "turned on the heat" on Martenis so as to be in Bethlehem next June. Be sure to continue, monthly, this heat treatment, and turn up the thermostat each month.

Kansas Miller is the second good fellow to send a subscription to the ALUMNI BULLETIN. He has recently been confined to the house with a slight attack of the grippe, but fully expects to be with us next June in Bethlehem.

Good old Empie seems to think that he is so much isolated in North Carolina that he has decided with the approval of Jim Burley to try out the Rotating guest correspondent idea. Much power to you, old boy, and you may rest assured that we all will do our very best to help you. However, please do not overlook the fact that many of the fellows feel that your outbursts of literary genius are more than worth the price of the BULLETIN subscription.

Next month you will hear from Fletch Hallock of the Smoky City and I am positive that he will turn on his famous xylophone selections to make you happy, so "wet your whistle" first and go to it, Fletch.

Your secretary hopes you will frankly give him your own suggestions and ideas for the success of our coming reunion. You may expect the first appealing letter soon after the first of the year. Be sure to make your plans to be with us for the memorable 45th.

We will miss very much more than words can express both Grissinger and Roller who were with us at our 40th reunion.

CLASS OF 1895

Walter R. Okeson, Correspondent
Lehigh University, Bethlehem, Pa.

Good old Henry DeHuff! May all his days be blessed. He responded to my call for help and so he is guest-correspondent for '95 this month. Henry has his own ideas about using a typewriter. He objects to capitals or punctuation. Far be it from me to take exception to his predilections. Here is his letter just as he wrote it:—

november 3 1938

dear okie
the last alumni bulletin indicates that you were up against it rather badly to fill up your space and perhaps something from one of the old boys may help out

there is nothing so dates a fellow as his college alumni magazine—he can put up a bluff any other place and think he is getting away with it—he may put out the idea that he is still on the bright side of fifty but not with you fellows

in many ways it seems only a short while since we were walking under the lovely chestnut trees that were lehighs back in the golden nineties but when i recall certain other things i see that we have come quite a distance since those days—for example the first time i picked up the bell telephone directory that hung by our old wall phone and now compare that thin pamphlet with the present bulky volume—that was actually several years before dewey came back from manila—then my old company had its first contact with the navy for some work in refitting one of the boats of the old white squadron—when i talk like this someone is likely to inquire what we had done towards fitting out general grant for his operations in front of vicksburg
those were the days when stanley de witt phil lovering and i used to get our meals on ridge avenue—breakfast 10c and dinner 15c for a three course meal and stanley bought himself a suit at lits for $3.95 which enabled him to hold his head up in his new job with the telephone company—we all worked 60 hours a week and felt good over it—naturally us old boys do not think much of the forty hour week
recently george buvinger '96 visited me at cynwyd—he is retired and lives in dayton ohio—thirty years ago he was centrifugal pump engineer for my old company—the d'olier engineering company—he designed some francis type turbines for us which were installed at the power plant at fort yellowstone and i have recently heard that they are still in service—gosh ding it all the stuff i furnish lasts a heck of a long time—mighty few renewal orders—the automobile fellows have the right idea F charlie bricker dropped into see us recently and last july eden called on me at cynwyd—he is engaged as a structural engineer on the new york world fair work—he looks fine and still has his stream lined shape—which is more than i can say—perhaps you can tell me but i know what you will say—dont eat so much and dont drink so much beer—but it seems to me that these days they make better beer than back in the nineties—the same applies to cigarettes which as i recall the old favorites of the nineties were horrible

now if you are stuck for something as a space filler you can put this in if you have nothing better—i felt sorry for you when i read your stuff in the last bulletin
with best regards to yourself skipper eckfeldt bob taylor and miss nelly murphy

sincerely yours
henry de huff
of the NINETY FIVE

CLASS OF 1896

W. S. Ayars, Correspondent
409 Engineering Bldg., Columbia Univ.
New York City

Two "change-of-address" cards have come in. The first states that from now on, Mr. Hobart Bentley Ayers, "Buck" to you, has no business address, but may be reached at 3 Maple Ave., Westerly, Rhode Island. As this is a long trek from Pittsburgh, I take it that Buck has decided to retire, though the card did not say so. The other one states that Bartholomew has retired, and that his new address will be Essex Fells, N. J. His old address was 120 Broadway, New York City, but I do not think I have seen him for a good many years.

A newspaper clipping has also been sent to me, referring to a gift made to the University Library by Joe Thurston. Being too indolent to copy it out, I am attaching it to this manuscript, and I trust the editor will find room to print it in full.

The clipping says: "Joseph W. Thurston, '96, grandson of Henry Coppee, Lehigh's first president, gave the library some memorabilia from his grandfather's library, Howard S. Leach, librarian, announced yesterday.

"The most important items are ten lectures in manuscript form which Dr. Coppee gave publicly many times. These are in Dr. Coppee's handwriting and are dated 1890. He gave these lectures as a course in the Old Opera House on Wyandotte Street in Bethlehem.

"Among these papers is the Memorial of the Board of Trustees, signed by E. P. Wilbur, secretary, and Nelson S. Rulison, president of the Board of Trustees. There is also a letter from Coppee, serving as second lieutenant in the Mexican war, dated 1847, to Dr. W. B. Stevens, later Bishop Stevens, first president of the Board of Trustees. There is a letter written by Edith Wharton, the novelist, to Mrs. Griffith, Dr. Coppee's daughter."

I also regret to chronicle the death of the wife of Bert Wilson, who died at Baltimore on Thursday, September 22. This saddening news came to me in a note from the Alumni Office. Mrs. Wilson was interred at Leesburg, Virginia. She is survived by her husband and four daughters. She was a sister-in-law of F. W. B. Pile, E. M. '88, from whom this information came.

Joe Siegel called up this afternoon (November 14) to ask whether or not I was planning on going up to the Lafayette game, but I told him I wasn't. I am afraid that I have outgrown—or out-aged—any desire to watch football games, even when one of the teams represents my Alma Mater, and the other her dearest enemy. Also, from such "dope" as I have seen, the prospects, at present, look like a pretty sad afternoon for the Brown and White. You'll all know, I suppose, by the time this column gets into print, and if my guess has been wrong, I'll apologize.

I attended the last New York Lehigh Club Dinner and was the only '96 man there as far as I could see. I was to have gone with Billy Dickerman, but that morning he telephoned me that he had to go way out on Long Island to attend a meeting necessitated by the hurricane that had recently swept the Atlantic seaboard, and he sent me the ticket he had purchased for his own use. Looking around me for somebody worthy of using this bit of cardboard, I ran into Bruce Johnston, temporarily in town, who got his M. S. in C. E. at Lehigh in '34 and then spent some time here at Columbia, teaching in our C. E. Department and doing graduate research, and last June was granted a Ph. D. Bruce is now back at Lehigh, and I think is an assistant professor. So Billy's ticket wasn't wasted.

There seems to be no further news, so I'll stop. No word from Pop Pennington, by the way. I wonder if he, too, is planning to retire?

CLASS OF 1897

J. H. Pennington, Correspondent
P. O. Box 159, Trenton, N. J.

Within the hall are song and laughter;
The cheeks of Christmas grow red and jolly,
And sprouting is every corbel and rafter
With lightsome green of ivory and holly.

I don't believe that James Russell Lowell had me in mind when he wrote the above; neither do I believe it necessary to remind '97 that it is now forty-five years since we went home to spend our Christmas, as Freshmen. Perhaps we were a wee bit affected by what is now called "superiority complex"— in those days "swelled head"—and perhaps we swaggered just a little, when meeting schoolmates of the previous year, who could not or would not go away to college. As for me, I could swagger on Sunday only, when walking up the church aisle, and hoping that I, as a luminous example of future greatness was being accorded due notice. During the week, I was too busy cutting feed, milking the cows, tending the horses and hogs, and a lot of other things, to do any swaggering. Nevertheless, going home at Christmas was an event, either joyful or sad as our first term exams were over and our youthful ebullience was either leavened or depressed by a bald-headed 6 or a mere 5.9.

It has just occurred to me that now, forty-five years after, I have a Freshman son coming home from Lehigh, to spend Christmas; and it further occurs to me that I am the only '97-er who has an heir apparent in Lehigh, or has had since

PROGRESS
ON PARADE

With 73 birthdays on its life card, Minneapolis-Moline knows something of the importance of fitting products to the needs of the hour. MM engineers pride themselves on sensing public trends. . . . Since 1865 many of the revolutionary advances in agricultural equipment have been born in the shops of MINNEAPOLIS-MOLINE and its predecessors. Plows, cultivators, planters, drills, threshers, HARVESTORS, engines, tractors—all have their chapter in the MM story of pioneering and perfecting.

The new COMFORTRACTOR WITH CAB presented at the recent MM National Harvest Festival and Style Show at the Minneapolis Auditorium, demonstrates again MM adherence to the modern tempo. Answering the tractor demands of today's farmer, MINNEAPOLIS-MOLINE has given him "living-room comfort" out in the field. Editors the country over are rightly proclaiming the COMFORTRACTOR the "World's Most Modern Tractor." MM KEEPS PROGRESS ON PARADE.

MINNEAPOLIS-MOLINE
POWER IMPLEMENT COMPANY

MINNEAPOLIS, MINNESOTA
W. C. MacFARLANE, '04, President

MINNEAPOLIS-MOLINE
POWER IMPLEMENT COMPANY

Digby Bell's boy graduated about eleven years ago.

Some time ago I received a brochure, the title— A Concept of Gravitation—by Thaddeus Merriman, reprinted from Popular Astronomy. I have neither the ability nor the space to review Pop's pamphlet, but it is mighty interesting, even to a lay man, and the most pleasing part of it is, to a '97 man, the very last statement—"I have had the important assistance of my son, Mansfield Merriman".

A few months ago, Hannum sent me a copy of a poem which he wrote based on the hymn "America". I cannot pass it on in this column, as it is indisputably political, but by no twist of the imagination can it be accused of glorifying the New Deal. Bud Saltzman also sent me a poem, which can be recited in any of Bethlehem's best parlors. This I'll give you, at least in part, when it has mellowed sufficiently.

John Sheppard bombarded me with post cards this summer, but not the bathing beauty brand. He travelled through the North Carolina mountains and was so rejuvenated as to be able to lead a swing dance. He still made me feel badly by telling how they sat before a grate fire and slept under two blankets, while the temperature in Trenton flirted with the 100 mark. John's writing stumped me, as this is how I read it: "I made first survey of three beers, then pre' heated my wheat field. Ran a river of Germans and many Indians without aid of New Deal". This apparently answers the old question "How Old is Ann."

P. S. The band still badly needs two more sousaphones.

CLASS OF 1898
David H. Childs, Correspondent
Camptown, Pa.

Mike writes me, between two busy days, to help solve the mystery of the banquet picture, and now there are but two unknowns, the ones on each side of Shepp. And Shepp does not seem to know, for my appeal to him has brought no answer. If I could only write two simultaneous equations in terms of these two unknowns I could of course get the solution.

Schwecke tells me his property suffered some damage in the storm that struck Charleston. There were five twisters. One of them was photographed, the picture appearing in a paper which he sent me. And up in New Haven, Jack Horner writes that their storm took two of his trees and the corner of his house.

Roots Daggett, due less to advancing years than to his labors as Class Secretary probably, is planning to retire at a time "not too far away," and will make his home at Trout Run, Pa. Then we will make a day of it in case the trout streams and tell you all about it later.

Your Secretary expects to spend two months, from the middle of January to the middle of March, in Buffalo, N. Y. His address will be 234 Saranac Avenue. While there he will fill up a column or two of class news from the Adventures of Baron Munchausen, probably.

CLASS OF 1899
A. W. Klein, Correspondent
43 Wall Street, Bethlehem, Pa.

At the Lafayette game, I looked about hoping to discover other members of the class but saw none. However, in the deluge which accompanied the playing of the game it was next to impossible to recognize anyone unless you were close to him. So here's hoping that several '99 men were present to witness a remarkable game in which the underdog—Lehigh—pushed the other team around in the mud, even though we did not finally win.

As no news of the class has come to our attention during the past month we will have to be content with the publishing of two changes of address. Jim Middledith's residence is at 103 Wetherill Road, Garden City, N. Y. The business address of Paul Hilken is Investment Securities, 420 Lexington Avenue, New York City.

Mr. J. I. Kirkpatrick, a member of the BULLETIN Committee this year, has suggested that the Rotating Secretary idea seems to work particularly well with those classes which have tried it. I can't say that the plan appeals to me as available for our own class column, but if any of you '99 men think it should be tried, all you need do is to offer to collect news of the class for any, particular issue of the BULLETIN and

we—the Alumni Office and I—will render all the assistance possible.

With the new year we must begin preparations for our 40-year reunion and if any of you have suggestions to make they will be thankfully received by yours truly. One of the first steps is the collection of class dues for the current year. Early in 1939 I will send you letters soliciting dues ($3) and asking your cooperation in connection with our reunion in June. In the meantime I wish you all a very merry Christmas and a happy and more prosperous New Year.

CLASS OF 1903
E. R. Morgan, Correspondent
Lehigh University, Bethlehem, Pa.
Nov. 1, 1938.

Dear Bob:

Have just returned from a seven weeks trip in England and Scotland which was most interesting as well as rather exciting at times.

While in London I looked up P. S. Dyer-Smith and gave him a copy of our 35th Reunion picture which I had taken with me to give him in case we should meet. Found Dyer pretty much as ever. He does not seem to have aged quite as much as some of the rest of us have done in the years since leaving Lehigh. Maybe it is the English climate. We had two sessions together and put on quite a reminiscence party.

I then went up to Scotland for about eight days and came back to find a changed London. All the Parks dug up for trenches and bomb shelters, and monuments and government buildings, people busily digging bomb proofs in their back yards and having gas proof rooms installed in their houses. Every one you met on the street (and they were unusually crowded) were swinging gas masks on their arms.

Mrs. Fuller and myself were instructed to go to the gas mask distribution station of the district where were were staying where we were fitted and presented with masks, also instructions of where (what bomb proof) we should go in case of an air raid.

Soldiers were all over the place. All steamship line offices, the American Express and the American Consulates were crowded with Americans trying to get out and all steamships were crowded to the rails. As I had my return passage booked and paid for before I left New York on the "Champlain" for late in October I made no attempt to get away earlier first because I knew there was no use and second because we are both more or less Fatalists and had the feeling "If caught we are caught" and that will be that.

I found rather to my surprise in talking to all classes of English men and women that the rank and file of the nation such as porters, waiters, cabmen, bus conductors, clerks, maids, etc., who would be immediately drafted in case of war were very anti-Chamberlain and very much opposed to his settlement with Hitler. They were all for smashing into him and all he represents right now and having it over with.

The older people and those who had lost sons, daughters and other dear ones in the last war, were all for peace at any price.

Anyhow I came away with a new and profound respect for the British Nation and much impressed with their preparedness contrary from what you read in the news dispatches.

Yours,

JACK.

CLASS OF 1904
H. J. Hartzog, Correspondent
Wilbur Trust Bldg., Bethlehem, Pa.

We are delighted with the responses to your correspondent's column in the November BULLETIN. Not a single complaint or criticism was registered. It augurs well for our reunion next June.

And now, here's an official greeting and announcement from our President:
"MY FRIENDS"
Class of 1904:
Will 1904 celebrate in 1939?
Answer. Yes. Thirty-fifth Reunion.
Has a start been made?
Answer. Yes.
The following gives you the organization.
General Chairman...........Parke Hutchinson
Treasurer ....Sam Caum
Chairman Alumni Day Committee... Frank Sinn
Chairman Transportation Committee

Herb Hartzog

Chairman Publicity...........Charles Michelson
(This is by special arrangement)
Mr. Michelson will be ably assisted by Kink Johnson, Don Packer, Frank Sinn, Herb Hartzog, Sam Caum, Jake Brillhart, Speed Clauder, Kiss Mussina, John Powell, Pat Reno, Frank McDevitt, Shorty Strauss, Jess Underwood, Mac MacFarlanc, and others, as the campaign progresses.

With Parke at the head of the organization and members selected by him, success is assured. However, it is necessary that every one responds to Parke's call to you.

Every member of the class should start now his plans to attend our Thirty-fifth Reunion. Watch the BULLETIN for further announcements.

"1904—THIS WAY" will be the rallying slogan.

Yours sincerely,
EDGAR M. MACK.
("Andrew" Mack)

Postscript:

"We do not wish to impose on the members of our Class who live in Bethlehem. I am thinking of Lew Farabaugh, Stanley Seyfert, Jake Beaver, Horace Cleveland, Parke Hutchinson, Sam Caum, and Herb Hartzog.

We realize that these men have done most of the work for the past reunions, however, we will appreciate it if they will write letters for the BULLETIN which will give all of us local color and information."

Well, there's your official notice and invitation. Will we hear from some of you in time for the next issue of the BULLETIN? Gosh, even a Christmas card would find its way into this column!

About the great fight our underdog team put up in that Lafayette game—sorry all of you didn't make the grade, even though it poured as never before. We wore out our rain-dimmed eyes looking for someone from 1904. What if our fubby fundaments got damp too! It was worth it. Now, if that article by Parsons, '02, in the November BULLETIN does any good, perhaps we will resume licking those fellows and some others by 1940. But it can't be done with carpet slippers and an arm chair aside a radio.

CLASS OF 1905
J. D. Berg, Guest Correspondent
Dravo Corporation, Pittsburgh, Pa.

My dear Bill:

The job you gave me of being a reporter for the next issue of the BULLETIN is more than paid for by receipt of three letters—one from Clot Brown, one from Pete Harrison and one from "Oom" Paul Cloke.

Clotty Brown, writing from 130 Midland Ave., Montclair, N. J., told me he became so contaminated with the Cornell spirit while running a 30 room apartment house owned by his wife, at Ithaca, N. Y., that he sent his daughter to Cornell and now has a son who wants to take Civil Engineering there. I think we had better have our next reunion quick in order to do some real work on Clot. After that experience, Clot joined up with Navy, stuck it out for a year, and is now helping P.W.A. spend the taxpayers' money in New York.

Pete Harrison has been Vice-President in Charge of Operations for the Atlantic Steel Co. at Atlanta, Ga., for 24 years; he has two children—a girl 19 years old and a son, Nat Jr., 23 years old, both of whom are married. Pete makes the horrible confession that he has been back to Bethlehem but once since 1905 but makes a solemn resolution to be back at the next reunion.

I am looking forward with a lot of pleasure to seeing "Oom" Paul in Pittsburgh some time during the next week or ten days, as he will attend a meeting in Chicago on Nov. 16th of the Association of Land Grant Colleges and Universities and promises to come back home by way of Pittsburgh. Paul is now a Fellow of the American Institute of Electrical Engineers, and besides being Dean of the College of Technology of the University of Maine, is well known in electrical circles on account of the frequent technical papers he writes on electrical subjects. Paul tells me that his son, Donald, was elected President of the Freshman Class in high school at Orono, Maine, the other day.

I had a very delightful visit from Russell Wait during September. Russell was on his way from Nova Scotia to his home in Houston, Texas with

Lehigh University
extends the Season's Greetings
to its alumni and friends

his wife and cousin and we all enjoyed the brief time we were together.

As my second son graduated from Lehigh last June and as I will have to wait at least a year to finish preparing the next one, it is probable I will not be in Bethlehem as often this year as I have been recently. However you can be sure I will be there in June and I am hoping we will have a lot more of the old bunch back then.

With my best wishes, I am

As ever,

DAN.

The Philadelphia Inquirer recently carried a photograph of Nick Funk and extended to him his birthday greetings. Nick is now vice-president in charge of engineering, Philadelphia Electric Company (since 1929).

CLASS OF 1906
N. G. Smith, Correspondent
Fort Pitt Bridge Works, Oliver Bldg.,
Pittsburgh, Pa.

The following message from South Africa will be of interest to all those who knew Van— and especially those who had the pleasure of meeting him and charming Mrs. Van on their world tour a few years ago—"Mandy" Lee, "Percy" Fyne, "Buzzer" Dean, Charley Gilmore, "Stepper" Gott, Lee Wray, etc., and Messrs. Anderson and Troutman, L. U. '08 in Butler, Pa., please note:—

Vryheid,
159, Celliers Street,
Pretoria, South Africa.
23/x/1938.

Dear N. G.

I wrote you some time back, but the letter which I posted marked "for Wagon Mail" (so that your son might get an interesting set of stamps) is not yet out of South Africa.

This year the UNION OF SOUTH AFRICA is celebrating the Centenary of the Great Trek to the North. One of the features of the Com. memoration is a modern ox-wagon trek along the old historical routes.

I thought that over-sea letters would be con. veyed by a wagon trekking through Natal, and then by ordinary post to the coast. As later transpired all "Wagon Mail" is being carried to the Monument here in Pretoria, where it is to be specially stamped—and then—and only then) to be sent on its way. As the celebrations at the Monument take place at the middle of De. cember my slow-travelling communication won't reach you 'till about mid-January.

Well, our elder daughter Violet was married on the 15th inst. to Ludwig Olen, a radio en. gineer on the staff of the African Broadcasting Corporation. He is about Van's height, and I trust he will make good as Van did. Violet looked very charming in her bridal garb, and I hope to send you her picture later. Her Professor of Pedagogy was delighted that she taught nearly five years as he considered her outstanding in her methods with the youngsters.

In January, 1939 my cousin and I are leaving on another World Tour—this time proceeding first to England and then over to New York.

Our itinerary is not yet absolutely detailed— but I think we are due in New York on the 11th of February. I shall call at Cook's Tours Agency for letters.

About five weeks after our arrival we embark from San Francisco for Honolulu, Japan, Dutch East Indies, etc., etc.

Oh yes!—We shall visit Pittsburgh and But. ler.

Kindest regards,
E. LETICIA VANREENEN.

Harry (H. R.) ("Mandy") Lee occasionally gives a talk before the New York Minerological Club—his last address entitled "Mineralogy and the Blowpipe Art." By reason of increasing neglect in late years by most of the mineral. ogical textbooks and much of the related in. struction the blowpipe art seemed worthy of historical review and appraisal of present value to the teaching of mineralogy and metallurgy. The address was later published in the August, 1938. issue of Rocks and Minerals, a monthly magazine of related interests.

CLASS OF 1907
J. S. Carlock, Correspondent
1301 Beechwood Blvd., Pittsburgh, Pa.

Once again there is a dearth of news from you fellows. All we have to offer this month is what the Alumni office supplied. Will appro-ciate it very much if you will take the time to write me something about your activities.

H. P. Dyson is living in New Bloomfield, Pa. His address is West Main Street.

G. K. Hertzog. who is Metallurgist for the Sales Development Department of the Electric Metallurgical Corporation, 30 E. 42nd Street. New York City. is residing at 130 Clare Road. New Rochelle, N. Y.

C. G. Shields' new address is 171 West 167th Street. New York City.

R. W. Vossberg is with the E. L. Phillips Co.. 50 Church Street, New York City.

CLASS OF 1908
W. D. Sanderson, Correspondent
Box 175, Pittsford, N. Y.

The Boss has gone out of town for a week. Usually that would be a swell rest for me. but just as he was leaving he says. "You gotta be Guest Correspondent and write that column for the Lehigh BULLETIN."

Well, I looked through his desk and couldn't find much except some postal cards and pictures of girls. etc., but I guess I'd better not mention these. Besides, some of the dames were pretty fat. I found a letter from Carl Baer who is running the North American Containers, Inc., in New York. He says he will give his per-manent office address real soon, on account of he is moving now. This Mr. Baer sounds like a good scout especially what he wrote to the Boss about "fox hunting." I hope I can meet him some day.

There was a note about a man named Banjo Bason who it seems got lost and the Boss said he wished the hell he knew where he was at. Can any of you gentlemen tell him?

I also found a letter from some wren named Mildred. (Of course there were a lot of other letters from girls in his desk but this one was the only one which had anything about Lehigh in it). Anyhow she told the Boss that Frank Perley was living at 751 Cleveland Ave., Eliza-beth. N. J., and Haldeman Finnie was with Lee Anderson Advertising Co., 8415 E. Jefferson Ave.. Detroit, Mich. Gee, but that girl must get around a lot.

In the drawer where the Boss keeps a little black book with a lot of names and-phone num-bers in it (wonder why my name wasn't in it) there was a clipping about Col. Philip H. Torrey in charge of Eastern Recruiting Division of the U. S. Army being commissioned a Brigadier General. Isn't that nice? I certainly would' like to meet a General. The Boss is only a vice-president and it seems as if they are about as common as flies.

Oh, I almost forgot to tell how I came near meeting that lovely Mr. VanVleck. I've been writing letters to him for the Boss for years and I think he must be grand. Well, he came up here and visited the Boss at his house a while ago. Oh, gosh, if only he had come out here to the office! Mr. Van has moved to 86-10 34th Ave.. Jackson Heights but I have his phone number in case I ever go to New York.

Oh, goody! A letter just came in from a Mr. Geno in Cuba. I opened it but I guess I shouldn't of. It tells all about the plans for the Havana Reunion next February. There is a lot of for-eigo words but mostly it seems to be about "senoritas." I don't know what they are but it looks like Mr. Geno must have a flock ol them as he is going to give everybody who at-tends the Reunion a beautiful fresh "Senorita" two or three times a day. They must be some kind of Cuban flowers or something.

I'd like to write a lot more to you boys and maybe tell you some things about the Boss but I've got a date tonight so I'll have to go home early and rest up.

With lots of love.

THE GIRL IN SANDY'S OFFICE

CLASS OF 1909
D. M. Petty, Correspondent
1902 Paul Ave., Bethlehem, Pa.

It seems as though each time that I start to prepare the '09 news column I feel the urge to apologize because the '09 notes have been ne-glected during the past year. I trust that for the balance of the season these notes will not

only be more regular but will be better prepared for I am about to ask certain other members of the class to assume this responsibility for certain months from now until June.

Aside from general news which has appeared in the BULLETIN your correspondent has very little to offer. However, I have. since writing the last notes. had the pleasure of hearing from Ben Campbell. not only in the form of a nice letter, but also with a copy of the "Columns," the magazine of the University of Washington, in which a full page was devoted to Margaret Campbell. Among other things which the "Col-umus" has to say about Margaret is the fact that her grades average 3.94 and that she has been elected to Phi Beta Kappa. Personally, I can also add that if any of the sons of '07 should happen to be in Morton, Washington I am quite sure they will find it quite worth while to drop in and see "Uncle Ben" who might favor them with an introduction. I say favor because from what the "Columns" says and from her picture she is not only a smart girl but also beautiful. I hope that Ben will not only come to our thirty-year reunion but will also bring his good wife and daughter with him.

Last June while attending my oldest son's graduating exercises at Harrisburg Academy the Headmaster introduced me to one of his prom-inent trustees who turned out to be none other than our own Sam Fleming. We had a very enjoyable short chat and for those of you who have boys to prepare for college I am sure that you will find Sam and his fellow workers have done an excellent job at Harrisburg Academy. Not only is the school well recommended by the Lehigh Faculty as preparing boys unusually well for engineering courses but also the general lay-out of the school is very good, and I have no hesitancy in recommending it to anyone. Con-gratulations to Sam on doing an excellent job in a good cause, but Sam, don't fail to send us some of your good football players as we need them down here at Lehigh.

This fall while attending a father and son gathering at the Hill School, where my youngest boy is in preparation, I ran into "Dutch" Boyer, whose son was playing guard on the Hill School team. "Dutch" and I had the pleasure of watch-ing Hill play a tie game with Lawrenceville which was the newspaper favorite. The boy re-minded me a great deal of "Dutch" some 30 years ago and here is another young man who I feel is fully qualified to enter Lehigh because not only is he a good football player but a good student as well, and as we all know that's what it takes at Lehigh. The other members of "Dutch's" party were his daughter and a boy friend, Mrs. Boyer being compelled to remain at home with a younger son who was indis-posed.

The above three instances indicate experiences which your correspondent has enjoyed in the past six months and I feel quite sure that a number of other members of the class have had similar experiences. Won't you please send them in. I will pass them on to the man who will be responsible for the current month's '09 notes. .

CLASS OF 1911
A. P. Spooner, Correspondent
1811 Sycamore St., Bethlehem, Pa.

Art Wells has issued a challenge to our whole class. Can anyone lay claim to being a grand-father? If not, the honor goes unchallenged to Art as being the first 1911 grandfather. If there are any other contestants drop me a line at once before the award is made. Art's grandson. Paul Robinson Bockman, was born on the 28th of May. Due to his remarkable physique he is nick-named "Two-Ton Tony Galento."

Art Frey was doing double duty last month— vacation and recuperation. Art and I held up the dignity of 1911 at the Lehigh-Penn State Smoker. Art had some very interesting tales about the recent New England hurricane. As proof of what he went through, he showed me a bill (which I am glad is his and not mine) for cutting up the trees that fell on his lawn, and also his hand which is not entirely healed from damage incurred during the high wind. In spite of the storm. he has decided to stay in Wor-cester.

Tod Rose didn't get back for the 25th reunion, but he was back last June during commence-ment week—so he and yours truly formally cel-ebrated the 27th reunion with a banquet, etc., at a little joint up the river. Tod is still keep-ing the Reading Railroad Company busy and lives at Wyomissing, just outside of Reading, but in a Republican township.

Just received word that Tommy Davies has moved. His address is 3 Grant Ave. He still lives in East Orange, N. J.

Sam Gladding told me he saw Charlie Koch in Philadelphia. Charlie is with the Atlantic Refining Company and lives on Cobbs Creek Boulevard.

Horace Kerr has been elected President and Treasurer of the Bayless-Kerr Company, Cleveland, Ohio. Horace also serves on the Board of Directors. As we have told you before in our columns, the Bayless-Kerr Company is one of the leading advertising institutions in the big city of Cleveland.

The last address received for Lewis R. P. Reese is Menlo Park, California.

Was in Altoona a month or so ago and saw Louis Smith in the Pennsylvania Railroad Engineering Building. Louie is counting on being back for our 30th reunion and wanted to know who of the other fellows were planning to be back.

If any of the other 1911 men were back for the Lehigh-Lafayette game besides Sam Gladding and I, they will have to excuse us for missing them.

Sam and I were so busy trying to keep dry, about the only chance we had to see anything was trying to watch the twenty-two nudistinguishable men chasing the ball around in the swimming pool.

If anybody asks you what was wrong with the Lehigh football team and what the prospects are for next year, tell them to look at last month's ALUMNI BULLETIN. If they don't have one, lend them yours and get them to subscribe so they won't miss anything in the future. Now is the chance to express your opinion, and if you don't like the way things have been handled, there is an invitation for your suggestions—so get busy.

CLASS OF 1913
E. F. Weaver, Correspondent
1601 Union Blvd., Allentown, Pa.

That grand old silver jubilee reunion last June certainly woke up the Class of 1913 and placed it squarely in the limelight. It's been a long time since a '13-er has been headlined in the pages of the BULLETIN and for that particular reason your attention was called in the November issue to Sunnie Edwards' story entitled "Let's have a reunion" in the previous one which was written for the purpose of handing down to posterity definite information on how to do a real reunion job. Of course we're proud of ourselves, hence, why shouldn't it be repeated? In fact your correspondent is beginning to feel damn proud of his job and is even beginning to feel just a little high-hat, but, can you blame him when he claims as much as a conversational acquaintance with the inventive genius about whom that outstanding article which appeared in the November BULLETIN was written. To our wandering delegate, Leon Mart, the class of 1913 says "We salute you." Just in case any of you '13-ers are in the habit of reading from the rear cover toward the front, and only got as far as the class news, take a look on pages 10 and 11 of last month's issue and read the "Success Story" yourself.

Doubtless you've read of the Annual Classic, the Lehigh-Lafayette football game, which this year was staged in a downpour such as we haven't seen at this game in many a year. The fellow pushing this pencil, with several other thirteeners sat, or floated during this typical but rather late "equinoxial" which our squadron pushed the highly rated Lafayette armada all over Fisher Lake. We had no right to expect any more. The old pigskin really looked more like a submarine than a football.

Bull Watson had such a pleasant time Saturday night that he doesn't know whether to send his boy to the Maennerchor or some other college. Al Gorman was able to identify every player on the Lehigh team from his number without reference to the usual program. L. E. Carpenter comported himself unusually well, but

he had his son and heir as well as his good influence with him. Hyman did not complain much about the weather. He wore a pair of rubbers, galoshes, two raincoats, an umbrella that shed all its rain on Sunnie Edwards and perhaps a suit of guaranteed rubberized red flannel under wear. Smiling Joe Parks missed our reunion last June, but got to the game. He looked much wetter outside than in, but had he been at the reunion the report of the latter might have read vice versa. Wallace, Ward, Rems, Smith, Beers, Bartholomew, Cole and Quincy were conspicuous by their absence, in spite of the rain. Some of the others may have taken to the tall timbers when the sky turned inside out.

Baldy Dutot entertained our reunion chairman in Pittsburgh Friday evening, the 18th and the guest reports that the lobster cuisine at the Duquesne Club is truly worthy of a Lehigh man, and more especially a thirteener. Sunnie called on Paul Reinhold also while in the smoky city and says the mogul of the Atlas Equipment Company has fattened up about 20 pounds since the reunion. He missed Sid Williams while in Canton during the same week.

Of all the interesting, enlightening, flattering or grouching letters received by either the Reunion Chairman or your scribe, the following from Ramon Camba, Guadalajara, Jalisco, Mexico is undoubtedly the most unique. Reference to our Spanish makes us doubt that we could do as well with an "unemployed" language after twenty-five years.

Dear Mr. Edwards:

I have received your circulate letter dated the 20th of past October and was glad to hear about the weather. He wore a pair of rubbers, of my bad English writing due to the fact that for a very long time I have not practiced it because have no often opportunities for it and have forgotten many words at the present, but nevertheless I am going to try to write in some way that you might understand me more or less.

It is for me really a pleasure to hear from, and try to have, any kind of correspondence once in a while, with my dear old class of 1913 of my

also dear Lehigh College. I used to receive several months ago, the BULLETIN by means of which I read whatever was going on in our College, but have not received it any more.

I don't know who told you my present address because my old one and to which I used to receive de BULLETIN, was to the National Bank of Mexico, in this place.

Perhaps you don't know that the Mexican "peso" is worth the fifth part of your dollar and that I am in no circumstances to able me the sending of value of the BULLETIN. If you could send it to me, as an exception, without the sending by me of the three dollars, please DO IT, and if you can't, DON'T SEND IT.

I have been working in a business of dyeing and pressing since 1928 and I am satisfied of it, even that it is not a great business but the sufficient to produce me the necessary for living. I was married in 1926 and have had five children. On last September died the only boy I had, at the age of eleven years and it has been a very hard affliction for me.

I am sending a "souvenir" worth nothing, but dedicated to my class of 1913, as a regard or estimation to my classmen. It is a sort of game used in this country and the form of handle them (they are two different games) perhaps you can find a Mexican college man who will be able to explain it to you. These kind of things are made by Indians living all around in our country (but not dressed with feathers as some people in that country believe or think about it). I hope this souvenir will enjoy you.

If you personally could send me some of the old Lehigh BULLETINS once read by you, I will be very pleased to you, because it will be very satisfactory for me to know what has been happening in Lehigh.

Please let you know to all 1913 classmen around there, that I am sending for each of them a very sincere embrace and that I will be very pleased to hear once in a while anything about them.

Hoping to hear soon from you again, I remain your very truly and dear classman.

(Signed) R. CAMBA.

And this all reminds us to ask—have you assisted in the guarantee or subscribed? Let your conscience be your guide.

CLASS OF 1914

Walter Schrempel, Correspondent
Artificial Ice Co., Bethlehem, Pa.
25-Year Reunion, June 1939

The following letter proved a God-send for this column. There are so many quaint and original ideas contained therein that we are printing it in full. The lad may be right!

Dear Schrempel:

You asked for re-union suggestions and I suppose you are being swamped with 'em but regardless, here are mine. Most likely they may sound revolutionary but then it appears that nothing short of a revolution could possibly stir the old gang into any semblance of activity. They remind me of the guy, sleeping in a burning house, who wouldn't get out of bed until the walls in his bed room got hot. Dead to the world! Even you fellows in Bethlehem have lost whatever pep you had, if any, as for instance, in the October 1914 column you promised to announce the re-union committees in the next issue. I failed to find them. Of course, if we are to wait until the last minute my suggestions will be wonderfully appropriate. Well, here goes but for gosh sakes don't disclose my name, for nothing hits the mark harder than the truth and I am still a comparatively young and healthy lad.

Agendum. Don't bother about showing up for the Alumni dinner Friday evening. You probably will see most of the local crowd—you can see them any time. Bob Mickel attended last June so that will be the last surprise we will have for some years. There isn't a chance of seeing Sanchez or Lopez, Bru Leonard or Lou Lacomb or Tony Bianco. What I mean is none of those distant chaps will bother to show up so why waste your time coming around Friday. And then the program is never very hot, a lot of talking, back-slapping, singing, drinking and all such rot.

If you think it worthwhile appearing at all, don't show your face until some time around Saturday noon about time for lunch up at Drown Hall. In this way you can avoid the congestion at the Memorial Building, the trouble of greeting old Classmates whom you saw too much of

while in College, and the bother of sitting through an Alumni Meeting—nothing but a line of goff from old-timers, and the foolish awarding of cups that don't mean a thing. The only reason I suggest getting to the lunch is because you must eat somewhere and this meal is free.

About music and uniforms for the pre-rade to Taylor Field. This procession could be easily eliminated and thus save the Class a great deal of useless expenditure of money and thought. It all seems so ridiculous, the silly actions of a lot of old men trying to regain youth for a day. Never before did I see anything so foolish-looking as that 1913 crowd in last June's performance. And they really thought they were good. Cut out the entire burlesque is my proposal.

With all such impedimenta eliminated I suggest that we concentrate on the banquet usually held Saturday evening. But not too seriously because many of the gang would rather stick around their frat houses, and quite a few will have to leave early so that they can get back to the Metropolitan area in time to play Sunday morning golf with some fellows they haven't seen since the week before. So after all why waste time on an elaborate banquet. Get some local organization to prepare a cold lunch to be served after the baseball farce in the afternoon and then with a few hurried words of greeting and farewell we can all rush back to the things that worry us the other 364 days in the year.

This entire program should cost us about a buck apiece. So if you don't return next June you would know that you were not missing much.

Hope these suggestions will help. If you see any of the old crowd give them my regards because most likely I will be unable to make it from here in Yonkers.

Sincerely yours,

RE-UNION IN JUNE?
CLASS OF 1915

A. V. Bodine, Correspondent
317 Mountain Grove St., Bridgeport, Conn.

Your correspondent has just returned from the Lehigh-Lafayette "boat races" which were held in Easton on Saturday, November 19. While the scoreboard showed that Lafayette was awarded the contest, by six points, I think all of us who saw that game were proud of the Lehigh team and the way it handled itself.

The only member of our class that your correspondent was able to locate at the game was Len Buck, in fact it was hard to find anybody in that downpour of rain that made the event one to be long remembered.

From best reports available, "Pinkey" Cranmer can be located by mail on Route No. 1, Clearwater, Florida. We understand that "Pinkey" is in the citrus fruit business and will be glad to supply the requirements of anyone wishing high grade products.

We are informed that Major H. L. Vitzthum has been transferred from Atlanta, Georgia, to Maxwell Field, Montgomery, Alabama.

We are informed that J. E. Bauman is now working for his Ph. D. degree, and can be located at 10 North 10th Street, St. Louis, Mo.

Major W. D. Ingram, has moved from Detroit, Mich., and his present address is unknown. Major, will you kindly report to headquarters as to your whereabouts.

G. R. Hukill, who was last reached at the American Consulate, Batavia, Java, has apparently removed as we had mail returned. If anyone knows of the whereabouts of Hukill will they kindly advise us.

Just as we are about to close the column we have a trans-radio flash from the sunny State of Florida that has to do with Perry McKee Teeple. Here is the flash—

"The United States Housing Authority has appointed Perry McKee Teeple, Lehigh '15 C. E., as construction advisor on Low Rent Housing Project, Florida-1-7 in Jacksonville, Florida, in the grade of Senior Project Engineer, Civil Service Group P-5. This reassignment by the United States of Mr. Teeple to more Florida Housing tasks is gratifying to friends who knew him in connection with the 1936-37 Jacksonville Project, also in Jacksonville.

"Perry is still the same cheery chap, industriously plugging along, and lives with his lovely wife and several children (they're 19, 17, 15 and 13) on the equable Southside in Jacksonville, not far from the contemplated site of the controversial Florida Gulf-Atlantic Ship Canal."

CLASS OF 1916

D. T. Wynne, B.A., Correspondent
5 Mill St., Port Chester, N. Y.

When I received the names of the B. A. members of our Class with the idea of compiling some interesting class notes, I immediately followed instructions. I had three replies. As to the others, I am inclined to throw the mantle of charity around them and say that there must have been good reason in each case for not replying to my request for news.

Ellis Brodstein was the first to reply. He was generous in his good wishes to me but stingy with his news. He did say, however, that he is practicing law at Reading and in his spare time improves his violin playing at which as we all remember, he was very proficient when he was at Lehigh. Ellis took his Bachelor of Arts Degree as seriously that he has remained a bachelor to this lay.

Eddie Clare has become a big manufacturer of some kind of cloth at Athol, Mass. He is President of the company which bears the name of Athol Mfg. Co. I say he manufactures some kind of cloth because for the life of me I could not make out what kind of cloth even though written in his own hand writing. My penmanship isn't so hot either or I would not have the temerity to mention Eddie's. Eddie admits to thinning hair and rounding contour and says that when he must be sociable he takes his with just a little soda. As a spare time diversion Eddie has taken to fishing and likes it.

Jake Hagenbuch was the other B. A. to answer my earnest appeal for news. Jake could have written his Thesis on a postage stamp and that implies no reflection on the Thesis. He covered the return postal card I sent him from top to bottom and a little on the edges with all the news from the year 1916 to date. It was mostly family news of interest to my wife and myself. Jake's sister, Nance, and my wife were Fem Sems together back in our undergraduate days when Lehigh Football Teams were more fortunate and perhaps more formidable than they have been recently. Jake's way of saying this is that he is still interested but does not bet on Lehigh Football Teams. He has one son in a southern college and one in high school at Newark. He is justly proud of his family which includes the all important wife who in this case was imported from Canada. He names a few of the Big Guns in the Country for whom he has absolutely no use. Then he O K's a few in humbler station and he picks them about as you and I would. Jake is still satisfied that he took his B. A. at Lehigh which helped to fit him for his position in the legal Department of The Prudential Insurance Co. He ends his interesting card with the familiar "Come see us once."

My own news is short and uninteresting. I am still in the Grain and Feed business which with the breaking up of the large estates is feeling the effects of the changing complexion of the community. My family consists of wife, Mary Elinor 14, Donald Jr., 12 who once in a while mentions Lehigh. My spare time is given to some extent to educational matters, being a member of the Board of Education. On Armistice night I was coming from the movies at White Plains when I noticed a face which I thought I recognized as someone I had seen at Lehigh. To check my memory, I said something out loud about Lehigh and sure enough he turned around at the name. It turned out to be Bucky Harris of the class of 1914. To my knowledge I have not seen him since 1914. His wife probably had the explanation of my recognizing him. She said there is something the same about all Lehigh men. She didn't say what and perhaps we had better let it go at that.

CLASS OF 1917

L. J. Breen, Guest Correspondent
P. O. Box 555, Hohokus, N. J.

I just received a letter from the BULLETIN Office saying I was "elected" for the December issue. That makes it twice in one week—because—"me and Barbour was elected" last Tuesday. After a few more campaigns such as this one, what a party we will have in 1942!!

Bunny McCann phoned last week and said he would be at Mealey's after the Lafayette game. W. W. Gilmore is a three striper at the Naval Base, Norfolk, Va.

It is my opinion that Stuffy Crichton disappeared after the election, because my letter addressed to "Collier's" was returned marked "unknown."

L. D. Humphrey is at the Park Works, Eastman Kodak Co., Rochester, N. Y.

Frank Mazee is Sheet Sales Manager, Aluminum Co. of America, Pittsburgh, Pa. "My Gawd, Mac, at your age must you live on Rosemary Road?"

Chet Kingsley called me last week (from a pay-station) because, when I called back the operator told me—"service discontinued for nonpayment of bill." Now I know why I got his job. (Note—for one month only!)

Sleepy Vreeland phoned last summer and asked when we were going to have a reunion. I told him "1967." He is calling on architects for the National Fireproofing Co.

Don Dosch is still selling greenhouses for Hitchings & Co. Here's a lead for you.—"Dream Cottage," Hyde Park, N. Y. Owner usually away fishing.

I met Rapoport at the Goshen races in August. After the main event I couldn't find him—now you all know it must have been a big crowd, ain't?

Goodness me, gracious, I wish I could finish this job with a couple of stories. Well, you'll have to wait.

CLASS OF 1918

By A. W. (Whitey) Lewis
As told to A. G. Host ....

Al,—says the boss, I have a little assignment for you,—there's a Mr. Lewis, an official of the steel company that's putting up our new supercolossal sound stage on No. 2 lot,—he's a friend of mine and he asks me if we have a high powered publicity man who can do a little job for him, so I immediately think of you. Sure—says

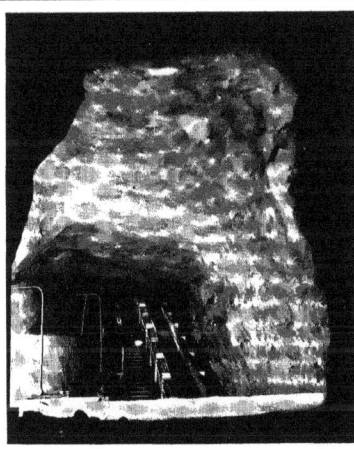

Although at first glance this might appear to be the remains of some prehistoric mammal, it actually shows the modern, lowest-cost means of transportation from mine bottom to preparation plant—the belt conveyor slope method.

In this slope entry, which serves as a combination conveyorway, manway and material opening, a Link-Belt anti-friction belt conveyor takes coal in a continuous "stream" to the preparation plant. It is 891-ft. long, with a lift of approximately 200-ft.

On the bottom, a Link-Belt electrically-controlled mine car feeder hauls the mine cars to a Link-Belt electrically-operated rotary dump, which dumps entrain, to a 2-compartment hopper. This installation has shown the following advantages:

Lower initial cost.
Economy in power.
Low cost per ton of coal transported.
Increased capacity.
Uniform delivery of coal to the plant.
Low cost of equipment maintenance.
Ability to use larger mine cars.
Longer life of mine cars.
Uninterrupted continuous service.

LINK-BELT COMPANY

300 W. Pershing Road, Chicago
Philadelphia   Pittsburgh   Huntington, W. Va.
Cleveland or Wilkes-Barre

Edward J. Burnell, '12   C. A. Woerwag, '10
Harold S. Pierce, '04   Thomas Linton, '34
                  Morris B. Uhrich, '33

LINK-BELT

MATERIAL HANDLING, PREPARATION, DRYING, POWER TRANSMISSION EQUIPMENT

7594

I. Well says the boss. this Mr. Lewis has written letters to all the members of the class he graduated from college with, (wenty years ago. Didn't think this Lewis fellow was that young, says I. Anyway says the boss. Lewis tells me that he has to get the column in the airmail east by tonight and he's tied up all afternoon with me and our golf foursome and I don't want him to miss it because between you and me Al. Lewis is a lousy golfer and I'm playing the best game I ever played, so I want to do something real nice for Lewis and I told him yon'd write the column for him—sec. Oh yeah, says I, so you want to do something real nice for this guy and I write his column, with all the new stars waiting for me to get their publicity out, to put them over, and there's only twenty-four hours in the day, now listen J. B.—Never mind says the boss you can have Lucille help you and I'm busy—get going.

There was a letter from a Joe by the name of Jack Beard, the fellow must be cuckoo, writes about soft white stuff that falls from the sky— states that he's a better soccer player than either Lewis or a fellow by the name of Tizard, that Lewis was tricky with his feet but seldom on his feet. This guy is manager for Haveg Corp.— chemical equipment, lives in Cleveland, has a girl eleven and a boy seven. Says he makes lots of trips like Pittsburgh, Buffalo, Detroit, Syracuse, etc., and he goes for his health (so that he can eat) likes tennis.

Oh well, here's another from a fellow Jack Knight—says he has a Scottie dog and a wife and that both of them give him a helluva lot of trouble and neither one as yet is house-broke and that to count him out as far as having any halfbacks to send to Lehigh, unless someone recommends monkey-glands. Says this guy Whitey was pretty good at getting the rest of us to do things for him, even to the girls at Mealey's. (Must be some girls' school near Lehigh). Knight states further that he weighs 180 and went through a change of life two years ago. There's a picture inclosed showing Knight with a tiger skin over his shoulder and a caption "from diamond mining and African adventure to an insurance business and a model home, is the saga of Jack Knight, shown above. Note his fingers through the hole in the 'cat' skin. The hole was made by the spear of one of his African 'boys'." He 'lives in Rochester, New York.

A fellow by the name of Weston Dodson, writes from New Haven, Conn. Says he is not president of his company and thanks goodness there is still a company. He's cheerful even in these times of duress, disease and Democrats. Has one daughter graduating from high school. Sees a fellow by the name of Bill Spear, a broker with Eastland & Co., 49 Pearl St., Hartford, Conn. Had dinner with another lad by the name Mizel, who lives in Kingston, New York, who has nice family with two kids—Spear has two girls, one boy. Dodson claims that if he remembers rightly he had a helluvafine evening with the gang at the reunion last June.

A Richard Alden (somebody is always putting that family over this time of year) is vice-president and head of research for the Phillips Petroleum Company.

Another fellow by the name of Latimer has a hardware business back in Pittsburgh. (I wonder if he travels for his health).

A lad by the name of Lawall is one of the head men for G. E. at Nela Park (that's near Cleveland).

Now look at the time will you—there were letters from fellows outside the U. S.—several from South America, one from Cuba, one from India. one from Japan and two from China and I'll bet all of them got along fine together when they were kids in school. I guess I just don't understand and time's up and that's thirty for me on this assignment.

STATISTICS SHEET
LEHIGH COLLEGE, CLASS 1918
By Lucille

Class Roll	144
Californians	5
Others	139
Living	3%
Married	97%
Children	67%
Dogs	33%
BUSINESS (Classified)	
Bankers	none
Barbers	none
Brewers ....(last six years)	none
Lawyers	3
Iron Puddlers	6
Politicians	56
Salesmen	93
Engineers	4
Farmers	1
Eat Regularly	43%
Bald Headed	67%
Too Fat	83%
False Teeth	48%
Flat Feet	59 %

CLASS OF 1919
F. H. Hesselschwerdt, Correspondent
Chamber of Commerce Bldg., Buffalo, N. Y.

When Joe Rosenmiller asked me to write the copy for the December issue of the ALUMNI BULLETIN, I readily consented because I felt that it would be an easy matter with all the information about the members of our class, which the Alumni Secretary receives. As a matter of fact, there were but two news items. One was with reference to Walter Park Amick, who is now Treasurer and Sales Engineer for the Eastern Steam Specialty Co., Inc., 125 Barclay St., New York City, and lives at 55 Mountain Road, Verona, N. J.

The other was that of John Knickerbocker. who is in the wholesale furniture business at Rochester, N. Y., and can be reached at 114 Croydon Rd., Rochester, N. Y.

Since we are to celebrate our 20th Reunion next June, each and every one of us should start to formulate plans to return, so that the Class of '19 can win the Reunion Cup. There are some members of the class that have never been back for a Reunion and it is the responsibility of those who have been attending regularly to bring the delinquents along. In the November issue of the BULLETIN, "Bucky" Macdonald emphasized the need for the co-operation of all members of the class.

This job of being revolving secretary or guest correspondent, is not what it is cracked up to be. Our class is allotted up to 500 words and I am groping for information. Having run out of material, there is nothing more to do but ad lib—and that means talking about myself. My business connections haven't changed in the last 15 years. I am still with the Cooperative G. L. F. Mills, Inc., a cooperative organization originated to furnish farmers with high-quality feed, seeds, fertilizer and farm supplies.

In closing, thanks a lot for the time you have taken to read this. I don't know who is slated to take care of the January issue, but I urge all of you to send in a bit of news about yourself so as to ease his job. You are all interested in what your classmates are doing since completing Lehigh.

Editor's Note: Guest Correspondent for January is O. H. Spillman, 46 E. Church St., Bethlehem, Pa.

CLASS OF 1920
E. L. Forstall, Correspondent
Penn Valley, Narberth P.O., Pa.

Hello gang! Station ELF coming on the air again. First let us apologize for the two months' silence. How did you enjoy the guest correspondents of last year? Hunton, Straub, and Bellman all did a swell job and it certainly was refreshing to read another man's contribution of news. Let us say further that Jimmie did an even better job than you knew for he wrote at such length the Editor was obliged to cut it down. So if you wrote to him and your news did not get in the column that was the reason. Then Russ Bellman was all set to do the column in June and wrote to about half the class to get material. He received some mighty nice replies. Unfortunately since the June number of the BULLETIN was dedicated to activities of the reunion classes his material could not be used. Russ and yours truly send their thanks to Bob Cope, Cisco, Texas; W. D. Schrader, Globe, Arizona; "Whitey" Lewis, Los Angeles, Cal.; Bob Brown, San Francisco, Cal.; W. N. Ryerson, Gainesville, Fla.; "Pol" Paret, Royalty, Texas for their responses. Gosh how the class has scattered!

Here comes a welcome letter from New England way which reads like a Californian raving about the climate:

Park Hill
Westmoreland Depot, N. H.
October 17, 1938

To Whomever is 1920 Class Correspondent:—

After several months of moving around I have settled down at the above address.

I was transferred by General Chemical Co. from Medford, Mass. to Marcus Hook, Pa. as Assistant Superintendent of their plant there, about March 1st of this year. They had bought out Mechling Bros. Chemical Co. for whom I worked since 1922 and I had thoroughly fallen in love with New England and small business, so I resigned in June to become General Manager of a group of Feldspar Companies with headquarters in Keene, N. H.

We mine Feldspar in Alstead N. H. near Keene and grind it in Keene and Trenton, N. J. and mine and grind Feldspar in Toecane (?) S. C. Then we also mine nepheline lyenite (?) in Ontario, Canada and grind it and remove the biotite magnetically in Keene. We have also developed recently a commercial process for separating quartz and feldspar from low grade quartz feldspar rock mixtures.

While in Marcus Hook I had the pleasure of seeing Merce Tate and chewing the rag with him. Also I have a 1937 Lehigh man working for me but otherwise I have not seen much of Lehigh men for over a year when the bunch were up at Boston U for the game. The boys did a good job of evening things up with the Boston crowd this year and I hope they continue the good work.

I live in the most beautiful spot in New England and see many summer tourists so if any of my friends come this way I'd love to see them.
JOHN TERRY.

Nice work John and we only wish we had known you were in Marcus Hook. It is not so far from Penn Valley.

And from way up in Maine comes this from Lloyd Fisher (known at Bates College as Dr. L. W. Fisher). He writes "I was married on August 26th 1938 in the Bates College Chapel in Lewistown, Maine to Miss Ermelinda McCarthy." Congratulations to the bride and groom who are now at home at 508 Main St. Lewiston.

Ted Estes called us up and we had lunch together last summer. Ted had just left Toronto where he had been for more than a year. He was moved back to Philadelphia by the Bedeaux System organization for whom he has worked for several years. Now we hear from the Alumni Office that his address has been changed once more and also his business connection for he is with American Associated Consultants at 11 West 42nd St., New York City. Awfully sorry we never got together for that game of tennis Ted.

Well, Merry Christmas to everyone and if you wish some more guest correspondents write and tell us so and suggest some names, or better still, volunteer!

CLASS OF 1921
W. M. Hall, Jr., Correspondent
The Hall Grindstone Co., Constitution, Ohio

Although you will be reading this a week or so before Christmas it is still a week until Thanksgiving. I am hoping that on that day I can give thanks for a Lehigh victory for we play the boys down the river this coming Saturday.

Here at home we are rejoicing for our Parkersburg High School team won the State Championship. (I was the first in years, that went from 'PHS' to Lehigh—then followed Rathbone, Langfitt, Roberts, Gerwig, Camden, Lockhart, Grogan and others.) Parkersburg, W. Va., is a town of but 35,000 but the 'Big Reds' "mowed 'em down" all the big ones—Charleston, Huntington, Clarksburg, Fairmont by a score of 73-0 and on Armistice Day concluded the state schedule with a decisive 33-6 triumph over Wheeling. In nine games won, Parkersburg rolled up 341 points to 41 for the opposition and gained 3065 yards—almost two miles.

Three trains—a total of 37 coaches—carried 3007 rooters to Wheeling and according to our local paper it was the largest football caravan in either scholastic or collegiate national history. Almost as many more went by bus and auto. Parkersburg is proud of its team—almost as proud of its band. The band of ninety pieces is colorful on the field—red and white uniforms—expertly trained and drilled. It is nationally known having received highest honors among bands at Kiwanis conventions at Providence, Chicago and elsewhere.

Would I be accused of treason if I suggested changing our Lehigh colors to red and white, having the best of collegiate bands, and a team with a schedule so that a majority of games would be won each season? Then, would we not find greater enthusiasm and support for Lehigh and her team among our Alumni and townspeople?

Capt. A. T. Wilson, Box 234, Bridgewater, Va. Last time we heard from Brick he was head of a CCC Camp at Petersburg, Va.

Walter H. E. Scott, Bus. Address, 356 Federal Bldg., Detroit, Mich.—mail. Res. 109 Rhode Island Ave., Highland Park, Mich. He is attorney in charge of Guardianship of Veterans in Mich., U. S. Veterans Administration.

P. Francis Weiss, 270 Commonwealth Ave., Boston, Mass. "Gynecologist and Obstetrician." Res. 16 Perkins St., Jamaica Plain, Boston. Pete led the pre-med class our last year (he was the only one in it) and received his M.D. from Harvard Medical School. He is a reader of this column so we can tell him right here that we all want a letter telling us all about himself—don't we fellows?

So long fellows—A Merry Christmas to each and all of you.

As usual Bob Billinger writes his reactions of the game, given below.

Rip! Ray! Son of a Gun!
Lafayette Scored — but Lehigh won!

Another moral victory? No Sir! Just an old time annual L-L Game, with no one winning except the weather man. Despite what you may read elsewhere in this Journal, most of us agree that it was a Lehigh triumph. The press prior to the game conceded us nothing but our linen. When it was all over the Lafayette crowd were so scared that they could scarcely arise from their seats—if you get my point.

The Smoker Friday night before the game was one of the most colorful ever witnessed. The Committee in charge had urged Freshmen from the various living groups to put on stunts—signs, banners, coffins, telephone-(?) booths, costumes and lots of noise. Prizes and competition brought a wave of spirit this patch hasn't seen in many moons. The kids really did themselves proud, although youthful exuberance carried many of the skits rather far on the Chic Sale side. "Bucky" Buchanan was the M. C. with a bagful of tricks and perfect cooperation from the house. "Okey" added a fine dash of fire in his best style, and also included a few over-brown stories. There's as much truth as humor in Frosh yells—"Keep it clean."

Saturday (Nov. 19) it rained "pitchforks and hammer handles"—as George Beck used to say. In weather much too wet for ducks, 12,000 maniacs, sat out in the bowl which Lafayette aptly calls Fisher Field. "Somewhere the sun was shining, and somewhere lights were gay," but at Easton it was Mudville and a sloppy, dampish day.

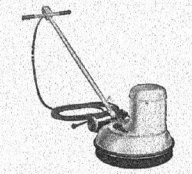
When you read Lehigh four first downs, Lafayette 1, you can size up the game—a punting duel with our man Smoke usually outkicking Moyer of Lafayette. Only one real flash of field running early in the game when Moyer got away on a trick 30 yard run around end for the only touchdown. Those long kicks on both sides would do credit to any team on a dry field. The Maroon runbacks of punts were better—due to the nerve and dash of the substitute Moyer (God was he good!) A slippery oval coming 60 yards from Smoke's powerful toe would be grabbed by this muddy Phillipsburg kid—and run back gamely through a sea of slime. The Lehigh band did a heroic and plaudit-winning job of splashing about, playing the gayest of numbers and forming hearts, goblets and L's with the snap of professionals. The laundry bills would make some of the old athletic boards turn in their graves. The band has won so much praise that some suggested that Pop Shields should coach the team a while.

The second half was Lehigh's. A freshly clad team in silver pants and white (not long) jerseys came out as if shot with a needle. Harmeson should have won his game on the sustained drives of his boys—the best they've shown this year. They tore, tackled and tread like winners, but never quite enough. No alibis. It was the kind of a battle the coaches promised—"win, lose or draw—one H—of a game." And as we came away we were glad that at Lehigh they still play the students.

Leaving the field I had a few words with loyal classmate Farrington, who saw most of them and helps govern the Phi Delts. He reported seeing Yelde and being with Herman Riebe. That's better than I did. I'm sure Shipherd was there, but didn't see him. At other games I saw Bob Good and wife, who boast a bright Junior Bob—a pigskin toter too, who'll make the team next year.

The Bartletts—Marie and Fay (adopted '21) attended the fray with Evelyn and yours truly, and celebrated afterwards. Next year hope to see a flock of you. Why not send us your reservations and we'll get a '21 block of seats. It can be done. Let's do it.

Please send Mac a Christmas Greeting with a word for the column. That would give him a real sockful. Another pleased recipient would be Henry Huettig—grand old boy of the Stock Room, who for the first time is on the bench.

From Mac and me—to all of you, Merry Xmas and New Year too!

Cheerio,

BOB BILLINGER.

CLASS OF 1922
John K. Killmer, Correspondent
769 Highland Ave., Bethlehem, Pa.

That "ounce of prevention" gag is a good one—at least, my preventative measures at the Lafayette game Saturday worked—for here I am minus pneumonia, which was freely predicted as a result of a thorough soaking in the rain. The boys certainly played an excellent game of ball, holding a team of Lafayette's present rating to one touchdown. However, both teams are inspired, in this game, to a brand of play far superior to that of the remainder of the schedule—all of which leads to the point of this letter. Have you read Floyd Parsons' article "Football Policy" in the November BULLETIN?

This subject has been discussed pro and con for a number of years but no one in the position of Floyd Parsons has definitely set out to get a cross-sectional view of the alumni sentiment. You recall our discussion on this subject at our Fifteenth Reunion Dinner; we all had a lot to say but in the end we didn't do much. Now is your chance to express yourself and to have that expression get across—so, write to Floyd Parsons at once regardless of your views. We can't all see 'eye to eye,' but I believe the class as a whole supports Parsons' ideas.

Don't forget! Number one job at the office tomorrow—

Write to Floyd Parsons

Here are a few notes about your classmates:

"Big Jim" Carey is now chemical engineer with the E. B. Badger & Sons Company of 271 Madison Ave., New York City.

"El" Daniels is still with the Dept. of Motor Vehicles at Trenton, N. J., but has moved to 15 Whittier Ave.

"Borax' Morgan gave up bridge engineering to tie up with the Virginia Chemical Corpora-

tion as Chief Engineer. He can be reached at Piney River, Va.

"Pate" Turry has moved from Hackensack to 46 E. Magnolia Ave., Maywood, N. J.

CLASS OF 1924
D. P. Hoagland, Reunion Correspondent
E. V. Bennett, Correspondent

1702 Cloverleaf St., Bethlehem, Pa.
Look out!!

We will be back on the "air" very soon again with all kinds of good and bad news leading up to our big FIFTEENTH next June.

DAN HOAGLAND.

Well, like the Republicans, the class column always comes back! I have finally succumbed to the prods of Ye Editor to again burst into print. The occasion: the FIFTEENTH REUNION of the now ancient and honorable (I hope) class of '24, come June the onest.

Fifteen

WARREN YORK of Allentown has been appointed the reunion chairman by FREDDIE. He will name committee members from representative district and college living groups and we are out to round up a HUNDRED or bust for next June. The banquet will be held on the second floor of the Bethlehem Club the same as last reunion and possibly class rooms will be reserved at the Club or Hotel Bethlehem for the whole occasion. We hope to keep the class assessment under $7.50 per and this will include free subscription to the ALUMNI BULLETIN for the ENTIRE CLASS from February to June (my pet gripe!).

Questions

Knowing that I can reach ALL of the people ALL of the time, I am compiling another class QUESTIONNAIRE which should reach all of you about JANUARY FIRST. The poll four years ago inspired 110 answers and if you stay with me as well on this one, I'll guarantee you plenty of facts and foolishness in the class column between now and June.

Page Floyd Parsons

The less said about the football season the better. Lafayette scored the points and Lehigh the familiar moral victory. Lehigh's present 1800 students certainly fail to produce the teams that our thousand did in the early twenties. Why? You've got me there, but speaking as a witness to most of his fall's disasters, I'm not inclined to blame the boys on the team for all of it.

Here and There

Saw STAN HAUSER and wife at the Muhlenberg game. He is still located at Pottstown and is a married man of two years standing. How tempus fuges, says I!

HARRY LITKE spent an interesting vacation in Bermuda and will gladly give any of you 60 families who travel the inside slant on the Onion Isle.

Our new FREDDIE ROGERS is the retiring president of the American Steel Warehouse Association, a job which represents large potatoes in any man's corn field.

To aid you question and answer men, please note my new Bethlehem address. The landlords get me down so I dove off the deep end and built my own. Do I hear any shouts of Optimist?

E. V. BENNETT.

CLASS OF 1925
A. L. Bayles, Correspondent
60 Wall St., New York City

FOUND: Al Bayles, Class Correspondent, struggling through the maze of the alphabet forest, worse for wear, but not beyond redemption. My thanks to Sam Senior for the well justified photographic dirty crack. Just for that he is condemned to be co-correspondent. That's rebuking him, madam. (Basis of a good story I shall tell on request, but out of the column.)

Last summer I was sentenced to Europe on a hurried business jaunt. While in London I saw Mike Callow, and spent a pleasant Sunday with him and his charming wife at their home, Dianns Cottage, Merstham, Surrey. The view from their home, on a delightful hillside, is one of the finest I have even seen anywhere. I have the suspicion that their pets would have to have two short legs to negotiate the hill in an upright position.

Mike is associated with British General Engineering Co., Ltd., Adelaide House, London.

Charlie McWilliams is Sales Engineer with the Marine Division of Johns Manville located

at 22 East 40th St., New York. Incidentally, he
sent in a two years' subscription to the BULLETIN.

Harry Finley is clerk of First Criminal Court,
City of Newark, N. J.

Walt Tyler is Development Engineer with
Tidewater Associated Oil Co., Bayonne, N. J.

Ed Jones is President of Edward R. Jones
Gasoline Co., 228 Brown St., Rochester, N. Y.

Whenever any one of the gang is in New York,
I should be especially honored if he would dark-
en the threshold and break bread. If the spirit
moves, drop me a line to tell me what it is
all about, or even tell me your troubles. I am
a good reader or listener. You will be reading
this just before the end of the year. May our
Christmas be a merry occasion, and the New
Year bring forth the fruits of good living, and
better luck with our 1939 football season.

CLASS OF 1926
John Maxwell, Correspondent
Lehigh University, Bethlehem, Pa.

There was a familiar face missing among the
'26 contingent at the Lafayette game. It was
that of one of our most enthusiastic classmates
and a real, loyal Lehigh rooter—Ross Broome.

As you may have heard, Ross was fatally in-
jured in an auto accident on the night of Election
Day. As secretary of the Young Republican Club
of Quakertown he was naturally whooping it up
over his party's victory and the car in which he
was riding figured in a three-way accident. The
shock was too much for Ross and he succumbed
the following day. Ross has been staging an un-
daunted, uphill battle against the affliction which
has so handicapped him for the past several
years and he had everything to live for. He had
been doing well at the service station with which
he had been connected for some time past and
the Republican victory would undoubtedly have
helped him along.

Ross was as staunch a Lehigh man as you
could find, as some of you were probably aware.
Despite the extreme difficulty with which he
could move around, he was a regular attendant
at Lehigh games and alumni events. This year
he was to have been host to a party of six at
the Lafayette game.

Yes, the Class of '26 and Lehigh will really
miss Ross.

A floral spray was sent to his parents in the
name of the Class.

This seems to be a bad year for '26· Last
summer, we lost Jimmy Morris, also by accident. Just recently the Alumni Office received
word of the death of Andy Ouss. You miners
certainly must remember what a great fellow
he was. He had been more or less out of touch
with Lehigh so not much is known of his work
and other activities since graduation. He had
been a designer for the Foster-Wheeler Corporation.

George DeBenneville is on the staff of the
Berlitz School of Languages this year. He has
been teaching at various places for some time.

Was out front, washing the car on the Sunday
after the Lafayette game when who should stroll
up but Ed Chew. Unknown to either of us pre-
viously, his wife's mother lives within a block
of us, so we can expect to see more of Ed from
now on. He is with the gas division of Public
Service of. New Jersey and is located in Camden.
He has a good size home of his own (heated
with gas, of course) in Haddonfield, a suburb
of Camden, one of those places you go through
on the White Horse Pike, enroute from Philadelphia to the shore. Ed is the dad of a bright
six year old lad.

Bill Miller is also with Public Service, but in
Trenton. He and his wife stopped in the Supply
Bureau recently to buy a watch charm. Both Ed
and Bill have been with this outfit since graduation.

Here's a letter from Jimmy LeVan, who always keeps us posted on his doings and whereabouts.

1650 S. W. 16th Street,
Miami, Florida.
October 29, 1938.

Dear Johnny:

The above address is my new one for all Lehigh mail; it is my new residence. Just two
weeks ago today I reported to the Commanding
Officer of the Quarantine Station for duty. I have
been assigned here as Officer in Charge, Aedes
Aegypti Control Unit. You have just read the
scientific name of the yellow fever mosquito.
This unit has been formed here to get an outfit
into shape so as to be ready in case yellow fever

should be introduced again into the United States—a real danger. The unit was at work here all of the past Summer. I relieved a medical officer who was in charge of it. I will be here for a while, just how long I do not know. I do not know where the unit will go next.

It was quite difficult to find an "unfurnished" house here because almost everything rents "furnished." Right now everyone with anything to rent is looking forward to the Winter season with its tourists. I have seen quite a few "foreign" automobile license tags, and a goodly number of them have been Pennsylvania tags.

Before I left Chillicothe I looked in the "Alumni Directory" and saw several Lehigh alumni listed as living here. I wonder if they ever get together. The University of Miami's football team is a big attraction for the two cities, Miami and Miami Beach, and the newspapers. I can't find Lehigh's scores in the local Sunday newspapers.

Now it is time to say, "So long."

Sincerely yours,

JIMMY LEVAN.

CLASS OF 1927

H. O. Nutting, Jr., Correspondent
20 S. Third St., Lebanon, Pa.

Your correspondent is very sad for circumstances prevented his return to the Lafayette game, the first one missed for a long, long time. Personal apologies to Ford and Farrell, (this saves two letters). I feel sure a fair representation from our class attended.

During the past month I felt sure some criticism would reach me regarding the style of the last column with just names, addresses and occupations of our classmates; however, nothing was received. So I judge it's something else you want, but what?

With football season over, we'll soon be able (I hope) to hold our heads high with the results of the wrestling season.

Is it asking too much of you, with the Christ-

mas season approaching, to drop me a card with some little message of yourself when you are in a card-sending mood. Seriously, I feel discouraged. You've never heard me plead in the columns before for news and I'm not now, only to state this fact: not one line from a member of our class for months. It's high time for some one else to carry on as class correspondent. Let's see, I took it for one year that was at least five years ago.

Let me extend to all of you the very happiest of Christmas Seasons and the best of luck to each.

REUNION
CLASS OF 1929

John M. Blackmar, Correspondent
New Vernon Road, Green Village, N. J.

All hail to Eddie Mittendorf! For this A. T. O. is our Number 1 man in connection with the budding Tenth-Year Reunion. Admittedly, your correspondent knows very well that Phi Delt Crewe, Sig Trautum, DU Kirk and Sig Ep Brennan have already said that next June they will be found on Old South Mountain among legion friends. Brother Mittendorf, however, is the first classmate to put in writing the statement, I quote:—"You can count on my presence in June." This sentence comprised the post script in his letter of November 9th volunteering several good suggestions pertaining to our coming get-together. Incidentally, Ed will have a long trek too, as his present address is 956 Greenwood Avenue, Winnetka, Ill. If Ed can come 700 miles. I guess most of our members who live much nearer Bethlehem can easily make town (if they only use their grey matter and secure the okay of the Mrs. well in advance—right now).

Wonder whether Ted Steinmetz will be on the scene. He too is now a resident of Big Ten territory with living quarters at Sheffield Inn, Indianopolis, Ind. Out in that city, Ed is serving as director of the Civic Theatre at 1847 N. Alabama Street. Some of our readers will recall Steinmetz studied the drama and stage

production at Yale following completion of his Arts course at Lehigh.

Then again, now and then, all roads lead to Bethlehem! Some '29-ers no doubt will drive back to the campus in snappy jobs in sharp contrast to the junky jalopies which they maneuvered around the "dangerous curves" of the Lehigh Valley back in the happy halcyon days of 1925-29, and en route will pass the Crown Point Motor Park (plug) at Thorofare, N. J. The president of this new super service station has written Billy Cornelius the following invitation:—'Should you ever have occasion to drive from N. Y. to the South, you'll pass my place on the way to the ferries. Stop in and get some gas, and if you are driving a truck, you can have a cup of coffee, free!" The president probably will welcome any '28' '29' or even '30 passer-by and most of the fellows from these classes will recognize the proprietor as Robert Bob Sax of Philly fame.

Returning from Main St. to Wall St. we find Benedict Boynton, called Carl by his Bride, employed by E. L. Richards & Co., Inc., at 33 Rector St. This business man is engaged in security analysis, which he does by the visual method.

Recently Marge and I had the pleasure of seeing the Yales play host to the Dartmouth Indians in The Bowl and we had an opportunity to eye-witness much of the Connecticut coast devastated by the hurricane in September. Knowing how many trees and poles and cables were down, we telephone men thought Jersey was hit pretty hard but I am convinced New England really felt the brunt of this phoney storm. Several of our classmates are living in this area and perhaps Ralph Read will be able to recount some stories when we next see him. In June? We hope! Ralph was one of those Leonard Hall boys who attended Packer Memorial religiously to prepare for the pulpit, and today The Reverend Read is assistant minister of Christ Church

Cathedral, 45 Church St., Hartford. Another Yankee, Ted Benton, is an engineer with the Jenney Manufacturing Co. in Boston but is living outside the city at Little Neck, Ipswich, Mass.

Sure, we also witnessed the Lafayettes outscore but not outrush or outkick a luckless Lehigh eleven on Fisher Lake at Eastontown and sure enough if it wasn't an exciting well-played game worth sitting through a deluge to see. The writer has had the real privilege and good fortune to sit in on every L-L finale since Hoddy Merrill's Men in White and Brown mitigated the Maroon's might in that memorable game of 1925, and even though the 1938 engagement was the Middle Three cellar scrap, it was a real fight worthy of the price of admission and of Bosey and it was the kind of sight that makes one appreciate "the spirit of Old Lehigh." "Smoke Gets In Your Eyes" all right for about all we saw was Sophomore Steve Smoke sending soggy spirals sixty yards for the astounding total of about two-thirds of a mile of punting, so if we get a dry day on Taylor Field next November we can look forward to some phenomenal kicking. Besides missing seeing Smoke, '41, you absentees missed seeing the following long list of loyal Lehigh lads, '29—Herb Bellringer, Roland Benner, Ray Black, Tom Brennan, Joe Conrath, Johnny Crawford, Bill Heilman, Jack Kirkpatrick, LeRoy Mendenhall, Tubby Miller, Gene Pelizzoni, John Carl Schell, Hank Sterner, Howie Wardle and Dewey Trantum, (the latter having cousinly-connections with the now nationally famous New Yorker, Thomas E. Dewey).

Larry Ackerman, my latest records show, is assistant professor of insurance at the growing University of Newark. In case you who just scan the scores on Sundays cannot place this college let me explain that it is located at 40 Rector St., Newark, N. J., and that this graduate of the Carothers school of economic thought is rooming at 502 Summer Ave.

Mr. and Mrs. John E. Jacobi enjoy a high-sounding address, to wit, Harvard St., College Park, Maryland, where Jake is occupied as instructor in sociology at the University of Maryland.

Eddie Blanchard's name always makes good news in this column but unfortunately while I have a new address for him—6310 Sherwood Rd., Overbrook, Pa., I have no information on why he ever moved away from Flatbush.

Anent our Reunion Committee, please be advised that the Brain Trusters (including two Phi Betes, a Dewey of New York, and one journeying Jerseyan) met twice in November and have made a good start on the big job at hand of planning to communicate by mail and word of mouth with each and every '29 man in our far-flung phalanx—not once only, but several times before June. First a questionnaire is being sent in December to everyone on our mailing list and we do hope a good response will follow. Remember, gang, this Class which holds the record Reunion for five-year classes is out to set another record by staging an unprecedented Tenth.

CLASS OF 1932

Carl F. Schier, Jr., Correspondent
719 Graff Ave., Meadville, Pa.

Our big news item this month is from Steve Baldwin, one of the Column's staunchest supporters, who wrote to me of his marriage on October 8th to Miss Heather Tompkins, daughter of Mr. and Mrs. V. D. Tompkins of Istanbul, Turkey. Though the ceremony was performed in Baltimore, Steve and his bride are living at 83-44 Lefferts Boulevard, Kew Gardens, Long Island, New York. A toast! — "For Happiness Forever," to the two of you from the Class.

Let's add our good wishes to Allan Ayers and his bride, who before her marriage was Miss Helen Stokes. The wedding was solemnized in Glastonbury, Connecticut, on November 19. The best of everything to the two of you from the gang.

Art Rohrs is now an Engineer on the staff of the Rust Engineering Co. of Pittsburg, Pa. That's mighty close to Meadville so you might drop in on me sometime, Art. Jim Wert is Assistant Superintendent of the Oven Gas Department of the Consolidated Edison Company in New York City. A brief note on Frank Murphy ties him in with the Farm Credit Administration in Washington, D. C.

News from Buffalo, N. Y. is that Johnny Holahan is a successful salesman for the Prudential Life Insurance Company's branch office in that

city, Phil Myers is now in the Research Division of the Valley Forge Cement Co., in Conshohocken, Pa.

Bill Elmore, who received his Ph.D. from Yale in 1935 is an instructor in Physics at Swarthmore College. Bill's home is at Yale and Swarthmore Avenues in Swarthmore. John Brown is located in Detroit with the Ticker-Waite Company, dealers in X-Ray equipment. Mickey Magyar has a clerical position with the Penna. Liquor Control Board in Bethlehem.

This being the last column before the New Year let me take this opportunity to wish you all a very joyous holiday season and a most successful and prosperous New Year.

CLASS OF 1933
Robert L. Davis, Correspondent
570 Lexington Ave., New York City

Well it's all over, no one wept, no one seemed disappointed. As a matter of fact we all feel that the Brown team held the Lafayette juggernaut to pretty nearly a standstill, or should I have said a slide still. Yes, no field has ever had so much mud on it at one time since the class of '33 battled '32 on Founder's Day nine years ago. In spite of mud and rain throughout the entire day, everyone had a swell time.

Bill Crouse wanted to know what happened to Burt Riviere. What's the trouble Burt, are the additional responsibilities keeping you tied down? You know we were all looking forward to meeting the young lady. Bill Crouse tells me that he is still in Philadelphia dodging swinging doors. Chip Dow is still selling insurance in Bethlehem faster than he can write policies. Bob Wall is still with G. E. in Philadelphia, and Bill Warreu is Vice-President of Warreu Thread Works. And how about you other fellows that were there? I didn't have the opportunity to talk with you as much as I wanted to, so why not drop a line telling me about yourself.

While in Bethlehem your correspondent signed up Bill Crouse as the Philadelphia press agent. Bill, we are expecting to hear from you en-re

the Philadelphia group before the next issue. Burt Riviere has also volunteered to keep us in touch with developments in Pittsburgh.

CLASS OF 1934
R. F. Herrick, Correspondent
Lehigh University, Bethlehem, Pa.

Rallying to the cause of '34's "Better-Than-Ever" Five-Year Reunion, Prexy Ben Bishop called me the other morning with plans for a meeting of certain members of the class to be held at the Maennerchor the night after the Lafayette Game. After probing about for any '34 representatives in that mob of humanity, I finally found Ben but so many of his key men had failed to show up that we decided to hold another meeting here later, results of which will be duly passed on to the class.

Ran into George Goodrich and Gene Wildman at the Philadelphia Club's football dinner and both are keen about the idea of the June reunion. George as you know is sales assistant for Westinghouse and Gene is air conditioning engineer for Stewart A. Jollett Co.

Got a chance to yell "Hello" at Ed Ehlers through a downpour at the Lafayette Game and while in the above search at the Maennerchor did see Clint Miller, Walt Miller, Jimmy Jobbins, Paul Short and Pat Loughran. We had one of those hurried confabs interrupted by people walking between us, around us and over us.

Prominent there, too, was Elbert "The Moose" Lloyd, from whom we received the glad tidings that there is a Mrs. Elbie, she being the former Miss Ruth Gardner Williams of Wilkes-Barre. They are now settled in a little apartment at 949 Hamilton St., Allentown, where The Moose conducts his business as representative of his father's firm.

Add to news notes of which there are so many that I could fill half this BULLETIN with them:

Bill Ridge is with the Morgan Engineering Company in Dayton, Ohio and maintains his old mailing address at 829 Washington St., Reading, Pa.

Les Weidner and wife are living at 142-20 232nd St., in Rosedale, L. I.

Vince Harton is the Northern Maine salesman for the U. S. Gypsum Company and is living at 198 Ohio St., Bangor, Maine. It will take plenty of gypsum to slay insulated from the cold up there, Vince.

Howard Hoffman is a mechanical engineer for Babcock Wilcox and Company and may be addressed at 19 Rector St., New York City.

Chopped from our last month's copy, unfortunately, was the good news that Ben Bishop had been married to Miss S. Wilma Steuer on September 17 in Packer Memorial Chapel. The very best wishes of the class to our Prexy are extended belatedly herewith. The Bishops are living at 1789 W. Union Blvd., in Bethlehem.

Bob Pangburn is a clerk in the bar sales department of the Bethlehem Steel Corporation here and may be addressed accordingly.

For you lads who may have missed the announcement, Bill Alleman is an instructor of English here at the University and is living at 533 Linden St. Bill received his master's degree from the University of Pennsylvania in '37.

Rollie English is now salesman for the Johns Manville Sales Corporation and mail will reach him at his residence at 275 Engle St. in Englewood, N. J.

CLASS OF 1937
Donald Barnum, Guest Correspondent
4 Church St., Bethlehem, Pa.

Since Joe gave me the job of gathering some information about the class of '37, I have been diligently procrastinating about getting down to business. However, Flip Fairbanks and I, who are living together at the above address and increasing the overhead at Bethlehem Steel, have seen several of the class at the Maennerchor and elsewhere, and are attempting to give you what we can. Much of this dope has been obtained from fraternity houses, so if there are errors, men, tell your brothers to get in school and keep in touch with their alumni.

First of all, let's start at home. Bethlehem Steel has absorbed Rudy Ashman, Ace Connors, Tom Hess, Dick Lake, (damn it, Walton, your typewriter still sticks) Johnny Lambert, Pat Pazzetti, Lou Pennauchi, Sammie Sprague, Ben Tillson, Jo Rossetti, and Joe Walton.

Rudy, you know was married graduation day and is living in Easton. Ace (dead wood) Connors turned engineer and is showing the mechanical department how to run things. Hess and Walton are Open Hearth men. Johnny Lambert will drop in on Bethlehem from Buffalo for Thanksgiving dinner; he's doing industrial relations work.

Pat Pazzetti and Margie Struble were engaged some time ago, and will be married sometime after Pat gets back from a tour of the plants on the sales "Loop." We saw Lou Pennauchi holding hands at a cocktail party last Sunday, and are sure the act wasn't due to the drinks, good as they were. Sprague and Tillson are in the mining department. We wonder, Ben, if the motorcycle is of value in your new occupation. Lake says he expects to be married soon.

"Cue" Ball is up at Lehigh working on paints with the Chem. Department, which is probably less important than the fact that he is living in town with his wife and small child.

Jack Gordon is Steward of the Hotel Bethlehem, and looks very happy and prosperous. He says he'll be in town for some time.

"K. C." Sloan is still to be seen in Lehigh Dramatics, and playing the piano with "Flip" at the Maennerchor.

John Drury is to be seen any evening at the Sun Inn. We understand he is doing graduate work at Lehigh, but his studies when seen seem to be confined to aiding a young Fem Sem beauty in her education.

Leonard Shick is writing sports articles for the Bethlehem Globe-Times in order to keep his comely young bride in food and clothing.

Although we haven't had a chance to check on this, the story is that Ed Aicher is also with Bethlehem Steel also trying to eke out funds for himself and wife.

Norm Halliday is working for Mack Truck in Allentown, and living at home with his parents. Yes, Norm, that was Flip and Don at the Inn the other evening.

Bob Reiter went to the Boeing Air School in California, and is now connected with one of the leading air lines at Newark. Abe Carpenter was out in California with Bob, and is now at Columbia University studying for a master's in psych.

Miles Harris, a frequent visitor in Bethlehem, is with J. P. Harris Well Drillers, and does some betting on the horse races on the side. He is at home in Port Chester, N. Y.

Herm Hutchinson is still in Pittsburgh with Armstrong Cork. Incidentally, he carries beer in his car with him on occasion.

When last heard from Abe Lincoln was doing insurance work in Philly, and Stooge Hildebrand was a Florist in Harrisburg.

All of Mo Lore's girl friends seem to have been married recently, so his recent raise with DuPont in the claims department is really of no use to him.

"Pecky" Peck, married three days after graduation, settled down in W. Va. after an extended honeymoon, to his duties as an official of—damn it, Pecky what is your address and the name of your company?

After a summer session at Harvard, Clint Stone was graduated on Founder's Day this year. We have nothing definite on his employment situation, but he is at home in Upper Montclair, N.J.

Ken Kennedy, when last heard from, was heading out to Oklahoma to do Geo-Physics for Carter Oil Co.

Dick and Mrs. Lord, we believe, are in New York State. Dick was employed by Remington Arms for metallurgical work at their gun shops. Hope that job was as good as it looked, Dick.

Ray Williams is at Syracuse, and while on the subject of that University, Pete Potochney is up there with au instructorship.

Pete Gretz, as we recall is connected with the telephone industry.

We saw Hal Dent at the Maennerchor last Friday, and can't for the life of us remember what he is doing. Anyhow it sounded good.

The last we heard of Harry Archer was that he was covering the Coronation for some American newspaper.

CLASS OF 1938
W. G. Dukek, Jr., Co-correspondent
536 W. James St., Lancaster, Pa.

Like most infants, the class of 1938 makes its debut in the alumni scene with a lot to say. The "white hope" of Lehigh, we graduated into Depression II with one of the gloomiest placement records in many years. But now Bob Morgan reports that over 75 per cent of this bunch is employed, and with business picking up noticeably all over the country, the future looks brighter.

And here are some last minute flashes from here and there . . .

Homecoming weekend and Lafayette weekend brought back surprisingly large numbers. Miniature reunions were held Macmchchorward. Chief topics of conversation were jobs and business conditions.

George "6point" Ellstrom and Arch Jamieson are working in metallurgical engineering in a steel plant at Latrobe, Pa.

Bill Sheppard is a mine apprentice with the Pittsburgh Coal Company. Hope he's keeping that trusty gun well oiled.

Johnny Frey, Baldy Berg, and Stan Rand, who spent a quiet summer touring Europe, walked into employment in their respective family companies.

Sam Felix, who also spent a summer abroad, studying at the University of Munich, reports from M. I. T. where he is taking his engineering degree that Cristy Conners and Charley Hoffman are some of Lehigh's graduate material.

In the marriage way is Kramer Schatzlein according to B. & W. reports while the number that have made the leap include Bob Titlow, ace cheer leader; Mal Simons, photo editor; Nevin Fidler, B. & W. news manager; Dick Murphy, and Joe Pittinger. Joe, by the way,

along with Mel Lord, Bill Getzoff and myself, works for Armstrong Cork. George Beck (it would be George) is a father for five months or more, and It's a boy. Let's hope he takes after his mother, eh, George?

Other vital statistics are popping up day by day. Apparently, a mere depression doesn't affect the urge altarward.

Doc Moore, last seen in the German American Club in New York drying off, after the 45-0 submerging N. Y. U. gave us has the prize job—writing publicity for an office seeker named O'Brien. Bob was quite sure he would lose. With a name like that, we couldn't see how he could fall to win. But we have heard nothing of O'Brien or Moore since the election. Guess the Democratic victory in New York drove them under cover.

Whitey West and Bill Gill are working with United Parcel in New York City. Whitey is in the office, Bill in the engineering department.

From the files we learn that Joe Kotanchik is working for the National Advisory Committee for Aeronautics at Langley Field, Va., while Ivo (Pachuca, Mex.) Kuryla is running the shoe business of United Shoe Machinery Corp. of Boston into the ground.

Red Blackler and family are now in Philly, letting Phi. Electric supply the weekly payroll. How's the future all-American, Red?

Still in the running for that job is Palmer Murphy, another embryo politician (see Moore-O'Brien) who reports seeing Cy Haas (Standard Oil of N. J.) and George Sheppard in his travels here and there.

From the South Johnny Weigel writes enthusiastically about his job as research engineer for Combustion Engineering in Chattanooga, Tenn. Round up the gang on the fifth reunion and you'll find John.

DIRECTORY OF LEHIGH ALUMNI CLUBS

Bethlehem (Home Club) P. J. Ganey, '10- (P); L. J. Bray, '23- (S), 1020 Kenmore Ave.

Boston, A. D. Bach, '17- (P); H. Lewin, '26- (S), 17 Pleasant St., Malden, Mass.

Central New York, Gordon Kent, '07- (S), The Kent Co., Rome, N. Y.

Central Penna., E. D. Schwartz, '23- (P); H. C. Towle, Jr., '28- (S), 3730 Jonestown Rd., Progress, Penna.

Central Jersey, J. H. Pennington, '97- (P); C. W. Banks, '32, (S), 329 Westmoreland Ave., Trenton, N. J.

Chicago, E. J. Burnell, '12- (P); C. M. Denise, Jr., '35- (S), 606 Sheridan Rd., Evanston, Ill.

China, T. C. Yen, '01- (P), 16614 Avenue Duvail, Shanghai, China.

Cincinnati, L. T. Rainey, '09- (P); W. S. Major, '24- (S), 1112 Chamber of Commerce Bldg.

Delaware, W. M. Metten, '25- (P); G. H. Cross, Jr., '30- (S), 2211 Boulevard, Wilmington, Del.

Detroit, G. N. Sieger, '12- (P); R. J. Purdy, '28, (S), S. S. Kresge Co., 2727 2nd Blvd.

Louisville, Ernest Klinger, '23- (P); C. M. Jackson, '33-(S), 111 W. Burnett St.

Maryland, F. C. Wrightson, Jr., '05- (P); W. E. Miller, Jr.,-'30, (S), 211 Hawthorne Rd., Roland Park, Baltimore, Md.

New York, G. R. Macdonald, '10- (P); Wm. McKinley, '19 (S), 414 E. 52nd St.

Northeast Penna., John A. Lloyd, '33- (P); W. B. Lesser, '05- (S), Clarks Green, Lackawanna Co., Pa.

Northern New Jersey, R. L. Trainer, '28- (P); A. H. Lasse, '35- (S), 917 National Newark Bldg., 744 Broad St., Newark, N. J.

Northern Calif., R. H. Tucker, '79- (P); A. F. Barnard, Jr., '32- (S), 3125 College Ave., Berkeley, Calif.

Northern, N.Y., R. W. Wesemann,'16, (P); Nelson Cox, (S), 1002 Eastern Ave., Schenectady, N.Y.

Northern Ohio, A. H. Bates, '89- (P); F. F. Schuhle, '26- (S), 853 Selwyn Rd., Cleveland, Ohio

Philadelphia, R. D. Warriner, '24- (P); Moriz Bernstein, '96, (S), 2130 Estaugh St.

Pittsburgh, J. M. Latimer, '18- (P); E. Stotz, Jr., '20- (S); 801 Bessemer Bldg.

Pottstown, W. R. Bunting, '07- (S), 349 Highland Rd.

Southern Anthracite, H. R. Randall, '23- (P), Rhoads Contracting Co., Ashland, Pa.

Southern New England, C. H. Veeder, '86- (P); J. W. Thurston, '96- (S), 168 N. Quaker Lane, Hartford, Conn.

Southeast Penna., O. V. Greene, '22- (P); George Potts, '23- (S), 536 Court St., Reading, Pa.

Southern Calif., Robert Campbell, '15- (P); A. D. Shonk, '27- (S), 1007 Cumberland Rd., Glendale, Calif.

Washington, D. C., T. V. Ganey, Jr., '23- (P); R. L. O'Brien, Jr., '33- (S), 1431 Manchester Lane.

Western New York, W. L. Lownie, '22- (P); J. L. Walton, '37- (S), c/o Carl Norbeck, Columbia Road, R. F. D. 3, Hamburg, N. Y.

York, Pa., B. T. Root, '06- (P); F. S. Eyster, '33- (S), 155 W. Springettsburg Ave.

Youngstown, O., A. P. Steckel, '99- (P); J. A. Waterman, '30, (S), P. O. Box 185, Poland, O.

PROFESSIONAL CARDS

Resources for an Age of Steel

When Republic Steel acquired the Corrigan-McKinney Company of Cleveland, it substantially increased its reserves of Northern ores and moved into a strategic position in the rich Great Lakes territory. ● Republic leads in the production of alloy steels—and in capacity for the production of stainless steel. It is an important producer of pipe, carbon bars, sheets and strips. ● Republic's new type of cold rolled tin plate mill is now in operation and a new continuous wide strip mill will shortly be completed, for rolling wider sizes than are now obtainable. ● Republic holds basic patents on the Electric Weld pipe process. An entirely new type of electro galvanizing unit for finishing farm fence and wire products has been installed in Republic's new mill in Chicago. All plants have been modernized. ● With such equipment, and with demand steadily increasing, adequate ore supplies are necessary—*and are now assured for many years to come.* ● Since its inception, Republic has been alert to the rapidly changing trends in industry—and, with an eye to the future, has followed a rigid program of continuous improvement and constructive contribution to *better products of steel.* Republic Steel Corp., Cleveland, Ohi .

Lightning Source UK Ltd.
Milton Keynes UK
UKHW021006161218
334046UK00008B/792/P